FESTINIOG
1946-55
The Pioneers' Stories

Michael Davies and Vic Mitchell

MP Middleton Press

Cover pictures: Front: This is a rare record of **Prince** in colour in 1955. The date is assumed
due to the hand painted crest and temporary wooden nameplate. (F.R.Archive coll.)

Back upper: The ex-World War I Simplex was recorded at Harbour station within the first few
days of reopening in July 1955. (G.E.Baddeley/F.R.Archive coll.)

Back lower: The Golden Jubilee of the launch of the revival scheme was marked on the Exbury
Gardens Railway when Barbara Mitchell repeated her original role. The cake carried a Roman
50 candle and a pipe through it which allowed the loco blower to be used to extinguish the
flame. (D.Mitchell)

> ## This volume is published 175 years after the Act of Incorporation of the Festiniog Railway.

Published April 2007

ISBN 978 1 906008 01 7

© Middleton Press, 2007

Design Deborah Esher
Typesetting Barbara Mitchell

Published by
       Middleton Press
       Easebourne Lane
       Midhurst
       West Sussex
       GU29 9AZ
Tel: 01730 813169
Fax: 01730 812601
Email: info@middletonpress.co.uk
www.middletonpress.co.uk

Printed & bound by Biddles Ltd, Kings Lynn

CONTRIBUTORS
Page numbers

PHOTOGRAPH LOCATIONS
· Picture numbers

PHOTOGRAPHERS

J.L.Alexander   K.Catchpole   G.F.Parker
G.E.Baddeley   A.G.W.Garraway   D.Rendell
R.Cunningham   R.Jones   M.Seymour
A.M.Davies   A.Ll.Lambert   R.W. F. Smallman
J.Dobson   V.Mitchell   J.B.Snell

INTRODUCTION

The inspiration for this volume was a letter in the Summer 2006 issue of the *Festiniog Railway Magazine* in which Michael Davies described in detail his visit to the abandoned line. Having had a similar experience myself, and read of several others, I realised that now was the time to bring together as many as possible such stories in one volume, for the pleasure of the remaining pioneers, for posterity and to raise further funds for the FR. Some have been written specially for this volume, while others have appeared in society publications. I am grateful to all these members who have sharpened their pencils or caressed their mouse and I also wish to extend my gratitude to those who have contributed photographs to help bring these stories alive.

The writers are featured in alphabetical order, with one exception. Allan Garraway's account is first for two reasons. His words give a comprehensive overview of the period and he was actively involved in the restoration from day one. He was co-author with me

of *Festiniog in the Fifties* but we suffered the inevitable constraints of space (although I was publisher). I hope that readers will find the individual experiences recounted herein add to their understanding of the adventure we embarked on into the unknown. Focus is on the practicalities, as the financial and legal issues have been dealt with in detail elsewhere. However, an exception is made by including an important piece on the Abandonment Order topic, written recently by Steven Murfitt, Clerk to the Festiniog Railway Company and a solicitor by profession.

Thanks for the cover pictures from the archives must go to Adrian Gray, Secretary of the FRS Heritage Group. Thanks are also due to Keith Catchpole, Michael Davies, Allan Garraway, Norman Langridge and Rob Smallman for proof reading. For consistency, the stock numbering of the new era is used throughout.

Vic Mitchell
2007

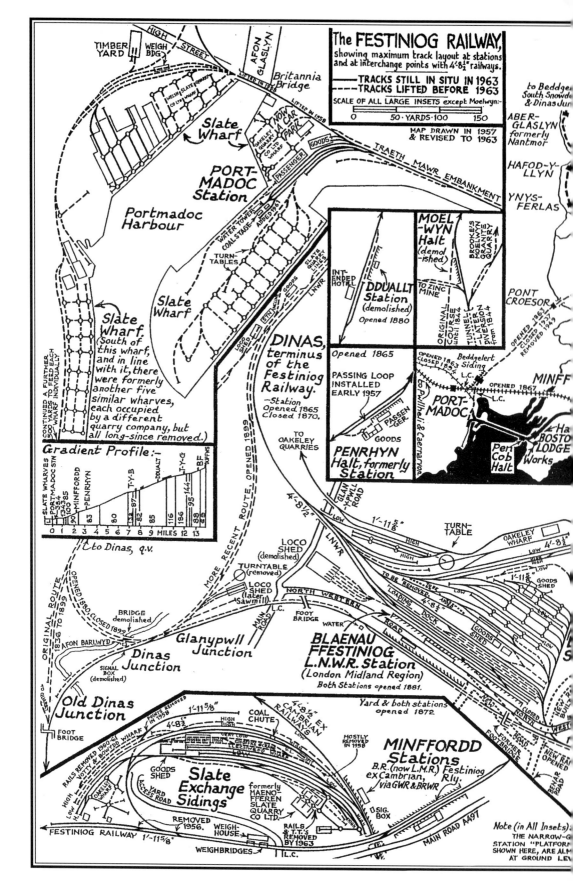

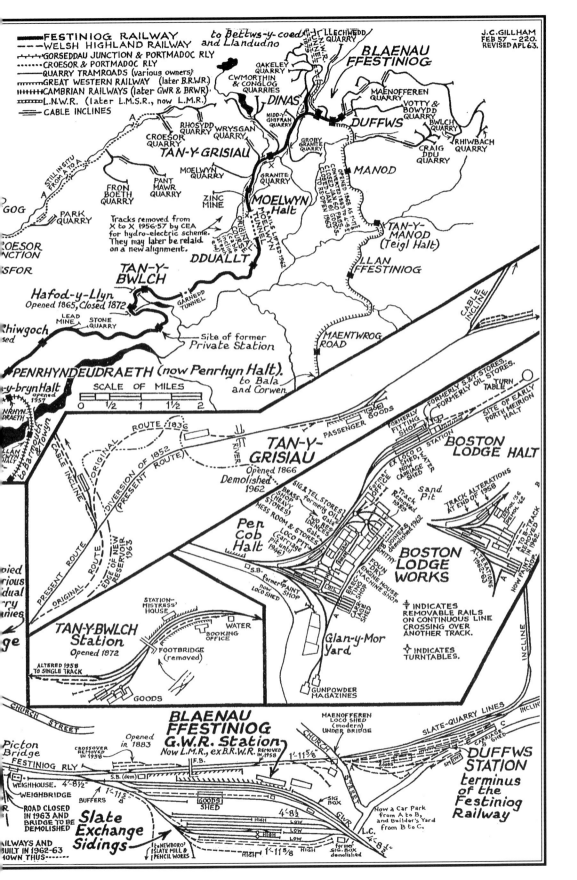

✿ Allan Garraway MBE ✿

After closure in 1946 various efforts were made to re-open the FR. Fortunately, as the railway was incorporated by Act of Parliament, it was not possible to close the railway completely and sell it for scrap without a further Act, and this would cost money which no one was prepared to put up.

One or two abortive attempts to reopen the railway had been made, but in 1951 a further attempt was heralded when letters appeared in various railway periodicals calling for support from interested people with a view to investigating reopening, and a meeting was held on 8th September 1951 at the Bristol Railway Circle. A very enthusiastic young lad, Leonard A.Heath Humphrys, was the instigator of this meeting and he regaled those present with grandiose schemes for rehabilitation and reopening of the FR, with costs running to five figures. The Talyllyn Railway Preservation Society had been formed a few months earlier to keep the TR running, and so the possibilities of running and supporting railways by voluntary effort seemed fairly reasonable. The enormous amount of work and cash involved in running even a narrow gauge railway over a few miles and the very limited amount of time and cash available in those days for devotion to such efforts were not altogether appreciated. Nevertheless, several at that Bristol meeting felt that though LAHH had rather got the cart before the horse, the FR was too fine a venture to be let go, if there was any possibility of revival.

The first thing was to approach the 'owners'. These people were the shareholders, as in any other company, and they were not prepared, and legally were not allowed, to let the railway be run by anyone else, except the Welsh Highland Railway Co. The possibility of buying up the WHR Co. was briefly investigated but found not practicable.

To obtain effective ownership of the FR required the purchase of more than half of each class of share. Without a majority holding in each class of share, another person could acquire control in that class and could make things very awkward for the Company.

As usual in railway companies, many of the shares were held by all sorts of people, in many cases untraceable or executors of people deceased. There were, however, some large holdings by a few shareholders who were approached with a view to purchase. The better classes of shares had a small value if the railway could have been scrapped, but the lower classes were valueless.

The biggest item in this was one class of debenture held by the National Provincial Bank, Portmadoc. When the WHR came to Portmadoc, the Britannia Bridge was widened and some track alterations were made in the vicinity, and for this money was loaned by the bank. As security, the bank held control of one class of debenture and the bank required some cash in repayment of the loan to release their holding of debentures, and this was about two-thirds of what it was going to cost to become 'owners' of the railway.

It was obvious to everybody that it was no use thinking of raising several thousand pounds by voluntary subscription for a moribund and closed railway. Moreover, the Directors would not allow the name 'Festiniog Railway' to be used by the Society. Considerable thanks are due to Mr Gilbert, who in those days conducted negotiations with the Secretary of the FR Company and, moreover, kept enthusiasm going when there seemed little hope.

Several people were approached with a view to obtaining the large sum required, but to no avail, until contact was made with Mr A.F.Pegler. He made an offer to buy up control of the shares - and become virtual owner of the FR - if the Society would properly constitute itself and support him in running the railway.

It was felt that this was the only way in which there was any hope of the FR running again, and in 1954 Mr Pegler became the virtual owner of the FR and the Festiniog Railway Society was legally consituted as a limited company forthwith.

An arrangement whereby a society puts a lot of work and money into a railway owned by others is clearly only possible with a high degree of mutual trust. It is a tribute to the character and enthusiasm of all concerned that an entirely satisfactory arrangement was reached whereby this became possible. Mr Pegler, having found the funds to buy control of the Company, put the shares so acquired into a Trust, the objects of which were the same as those of the Society, namely to preserve the railway. The Trustees appointed by Mr Pegler were Mr E.J.Routly, Vice-Chairman of the Company, Mr H.T.S.Bailey, Director of both the Company and the Society, Lt. Col. H.Rudgard, OBE, T.D, Chairman of the Society until his death in March 1958 and Mr R.H.R.Garraway, Director and Treasurer of the Society. Furthermore, an agreement was signed between the Company and the FR Society Ltd. setting out the future relationship between the two bodies in such a way as to ensure that they would both work to the common objective of securing the future of the railway.

This was the first hurdle overcome, but in the takeover from the bank all overdrafts, etc., were wiped out and a new bank account opened. There was a limited income from various rents, etc., but there were also several liabilities which continued to need payments. However, in the summer of 1954, a limited start was made by some boys from St. Paul's School in North London, who exposed the track to view from Boston Lodge to the Cemetery for the first time for some years.

During August, Col. McMullen, one of the Ministry of Transport Inspecting Officers, walked the length of the line, on a very wet day, and gave his opinions on our scheme. He pointed out that there was a tremendous task ahead but he wished us good luck as the very fine engineering of the railway made it a very worthwhile venture. He also pointed out that the responsibility for safety, etc., entirely rested with the railway company and, due to the nature and construction of the line, considerable care would have to be taken in all aspects of train operation. It was not a place where liberties could be taken and inexperienced people let loose without close supervision.

In September, Morris Jones, the FR's last Fitter, together with Messrs Garraway and Harvey, entered Boston Lodge. With only minor overhauling, cleaning of ignition and fuel systems etc., Simplex tractor was got working and some clearing up of all the derelict stock in the works and yards was done. On Thursday, 23rd September 1954, a train consisting of No. 10 and No. 17 was hauled out of the carriage shed and the local press given a ride across the Cob. A picture of this train was used in the Society's first Newsletter. Money was a very urgent requirement and arrangements were therefore made with a scrap dealer to cut up many of the derelict wagons etc., in the Harbour Station and at Boston Lodge. This not only raised some cash but cleaned up the place so that it became possible to move.

A few people managed to get down at weekends and work was concentrated on opening up the route. The first task was to shore up the track between Boston Lodge station and the turntable, where the bank had slipped, leaving the rails suspended in mid-air. After this it was found that Simplex made an excellent bulldozer, and with the aid of well-sanded rails, the brambles and bushes yielded to its repeated charges. Minffordd level crossing and the occupation crossing by the weighbridge took some digging out, but on 6th November a field day was held in honour of Mr Evans, the Manager of the railway, who had completed 60 years' service and No. 17 and No. 10 were taken up to Minffordd and run back with all the guests to Portmadoc.

November 1954 saw the launching of the public appeal for subscription to the Society. This also brought in considerable numbers of volunteers prepared to assist in various ways. This appeal brought in £300 and further money then dribbled in slowly. The approach of Christmas was undoubtedly a deterrent to many.

The first officially advertised working party early in December saw about a dozen volunteers and, with the aid of the temperamental Simplex, a way was made to about mile post 5½. Trees had fallen down on the line and these were cut up and hauled out, and then some stumps were hauled out by the roots. The sodden ground was a great asset to getting them out, but the greatest difficulty was manhandling the roots off the track through a gateway into the woods. We pulled down a sizeable tree and disposed of it over an embankment.

Mr Ian Smart had offered to rebuild the ex-Welsh Highland platelayers trolley which stood outside the Erecting Shop, and we dragged this on to the rails and round to the loco shed, where we loaded it up on to Ian's lorry. This machine had a reversible two-stroke engine. When it returned it had a two-cylinder horizontally opposed four-stroke. Nicknamed *Busta*, it had its uses, but it had many weaknesses and an improved version was planned.

Morris Jones and his apprentice, Arwyn Morgan, started full-time work at about Christmastime and were getting the Shops working again. They were hampered by the short hours of daylight, but had succeeded in getting the Crossley oil engine running so that the machinery could be used. Again, they were held up through having no water supply for cooling purposes, so that they could not keep it running for any long period. They were primarily engaged on rebuilding *Prince*.

The 8th and 9th January 1955 saw a large gang of volunteers at work and all the rest of the trees, etc., were cleared so that the line was declared passable. A BBC Television cameraman took shots of people at work in the Works and clearing the line, and these were subsequently shown in Children's Newsreel.

On this occasion Simplex's No. 2 big end had run hot, due apparently to the bearing coming slack, two of the four bolts being missing. Due to ignorance of the engine's construction, attempts at line-side repairs failed and had to be resumed next day. The big end was temporarily assembled, but on the return journey again came adrift, bending the conn rod and breaking the piston, but fortunately doing nothing serious. However, it enabled the engine to be run on three cylinders.

Busta came back on 22nd January and hauled a platelayers' trolley of people up to the tunnel, the first train to get so far. Much stonework had to be cleared from under the shafts before anything could run through. We were fortunate in managing to obtain spares for Simplex and it was again running by the end of January, when, on the 31st, it ran light engine to Glan-y-Pwll.

On 5th February Simplex and No. 1 van went to Blaenau for reconnaissance of the line with CEA officials, and also succeeded in getting through to the old LNW station. On the same date electricity was connected at Boston Lodge, which had been wired up by some volunteers from South Wales.

Simplex is a most uneconomical engine, particularly with modern petrol prices, and attempts were made to run it on TVO. By means of warming the fuel and air this was quite satisfactorily achieved.

The final stage in the initial clearing took place on March 5th, when coach no. 17 and van no. 1 were successfully taken right through to Blaenau. Although the track was still far from clear, it could be said to be again passable throughout.

Once the most interesting job of blazing a trail had been completed, the work was concentrated on getting things ready for operating a service that summer. The first bit of track work was the filling in of the slip at Boston Lodge and re-sleepering the track over it. Boston Lodge station site was cleared and the nameboards for it and Portmadoc painted and erected. Re-sleepering on the curve at Boston Lodge and then across the Cob proceeded, assisted by Will Jones at weekends. Work was very slow, and by the time services had started only the absolute minimum had been done. The track on the Cob was some of the worst anywhere and was the cause of much anxiety until it had been practically completely re-sleepered - not only were the sleepers very poor, but the rails were very weak.

No. 23, the ex-Welsh Highland Railway open 3rd, was the first coach to be returned to traffic, followed by No. 12. They were painted green, with ivory top panels, red ends and seats, with grey interior.

At the beginning of June 1955 I took over as Manager and Mr Robert Evans retired. Unfortunately, the process of handing over was made somewhat difficult as Mrs Evans died the day afterwards.

Work on *Prince* was accelerated, and Morris Jones and Arwyn Morgan worked long hours to get it running. Eventually it was decided to advise the Ministry of Transport that we were proposing to re-open on Saturday, 23rd July, and Col. McMullen made his inspection from Portmadoc to Boston Lodge on 21st July.

Prince was not ready, in spite of having additional temporary staff to assist, and the Simplex worked the shuttle service for the first few days. On the first August Monday the magneto gave trouble, and the service was a bit fitful on Monday afernoon and Tuesday. The official opening had been held on Friday, 29th July, when Miss Janet Jones, the Welsh Tourist Queen, arrived in Portmadoc from Boston Lodge on our train.

On Tuesday evening, 2nd August, almost nine years to the day since *Princess* had last run, *Prince* steamed across the Cob for the first time. Several trial runs were made to test the track, and on Wednesday morning *Prince* took over the passenger trains. After some slight teething troubles, when Simplex took over, *Prince* finally went into regular service on Friday, 5th August, and worked every passenger train until *Taliesin* came out in September 1956.

The service in 1955 consisted of two morning and four afternoon trains. As there is no loop at Boston Lodge, running round of the train had to be done at Pen Cob by means of a chain shunt, a tricky operation which fortunately never failed (too badly).

One of the Inspecting Officer's observations was about the pill box at Pen Cob. He advised us to remove it as no one appeared to own it; the walls soon crumbled away when attacked. The reinforced concrete roof, however, proved a more formidable task.

The service ended on 24th September, by which time there had been over 11,000 bookings, or about 20,000 passenger journeys. It had been a somewhat alfresco affair, but at least it had made a start.

During the winter of 1955-56 the working parties got better organised, particularly the Midland Group, who regularly sent parties down monthly. Unfortunately, during this period, cash was extremely tight and much time had to be spent on cutting up redundant wagons for scrap, many working parties being spent on loading this up on to British Railways wagons. However, the complete clearance of the Boston Lodge-Minffordd section was accomplished, albeit the last bit only a few days before Col. Mc Mullen's inspection.

During this winter, a quantity of ancillary work was accomplished. The old carriage pit in Boston Lodge Works Yard had become highly dangerous and had to be completely dug out and a new reinforced concrete pit constructed. A completely new water supply system had to be put in with a new pipeline from above the toll gate into the erecting shop. Similarly, at Portmadoc, a tank had to be erected on the staging by the three-way points and a pipeline put in from the main road.

The sunken road at Minffordd was dug out - almost excavated anew - yielding over 50 wagons, some for use but mostly for scrap, but also enabling the coal chute to be used, considerably facilitating the unloading of coal. At this time it was discovered that British Railways were planning to take up much of their track at Minffordd, a scheme agreed when the FR seemed completely dead. After pointing out that under the terms of old agreements any alterations to the yard would be by mutual consent, a re-alignment of the tracks was agreed upon, retaining all the facilities we required in one long siding.

In connection with the scrap drive, two or three trips were made through to Blaenau to bring down scrap wagons not used by the quarries. Before the CEA scheme started and our track was lifted at various points, also to assist in the financial difficulties, the flat-bottomed track materials on the Dinas branch were sold to Cohens, and the track was lifted at about Christmastime, 1955.

Morris Jones returned for a few weeks in the autumn to finish off several outstanding jobs on *Prince*, particularly the piping for the right-hand injector, and during the winter volunteers re-built the tender.

1. Harbour Station was seldom photographed from a distance in the closure period. One upper office remained in use. (KC coll.)

2. This 1952 view was also from a less common angle. The area had been used for storage since September 1939. (DR)

3. At the extremity of the running lines were stub points seen in 1954 along with fishing nets drying on the water tower frame. (RWFS)

4. A closer shot of the frame in 1952 includes the three-position slotted signal, plus more lobster pots. (DR)

✑ John Bate ✒

A family holiday at Borth y Gest, near Portmadoc in September 1950 enabled me to make a fairly thorough exploration of the FR and other lines in that area. I found my way into Boston Lodge Works and to the Carriage Shed through a hole at the rear and was also able to enter the engine shed quite easily. I was recommended to seek out the Rev Timmy Phillips but he was not at home.

I measured rails on the Cob for wear and poked my penknife into many rotten sleepers, also noting the almost complete absence of keys from the chairs. Some of the track was accessible but much was very overgrown and difficult for walking. I did not pay much attention to the locomotives or rolling stock apart from trying to count the huge number of slate wagons lying around, but I did note a rotten shed-roof-beam resting on a carriage. Another visitor to the sheds produced a copy of James Boyd's recently published book *Narrow Gauge Rails to Portmadoc*. I ordered a copy on return from holiday.

As there was obviously a lot of interest in the FR I was not surprised to read a letter from L.A.Heath Humphrys which appeared in *Trains Illustrated* in March 1951 and immediately wrote to him. I then became involved with the Talyllyn and my next contact with the FR people was the Bristol meeting on September 8th 1951. My diary sheds no light on the proceedings, merely noting the time I arrived at and departed from the meeting, which was held in a small basement room at the Bristol Railway Circle, which was a long walk from the station. I recall that a dozen or so people had assembled in the room but there was no sign of Heath Humphrys. After about half an hour a youthful figure appeared and proceedings began. Matters which were discussed included the state of the physical assets and the legal position of the Festiniog Railway Company. Heath Humphrys was expecting shortly to be called up for National Service and arranged to hand over his papers to a Mr Rear who, I believe, lived at Waunfawr.

I subsequently attended two meetings held at the "Old Bull" at Barnet called by Fred Gilbert who, concerned by the lack of action by Mr Rear, had obtained the addresses of those who had attended the Bristol meeting. I kept no notes of the first meeting, held on October 7th 1951, but I did make notes at the meeting held on December 16th where there were thirteen people. The main topic was an explanation of the legal procedures required to obtain control of the FR Company. Fred Gilbert's solicitor friend Taylor Harris had been busy since the previous meeting and it was now obvious that the only way forward was to set about acquiring a controlling interest in the shares of the FR Company. There was a brief mention of the earlier efforts of James Boyd to acquire the Company.

It was agreed that it would be premature to form a General Committee or initiate publicity at present. However, I was requested to prepare a covering estimate for the cost of essential work on the permanent way and buildings and Allan Garraway would likewise estimate the cost of work required on the locomotives and rolling stock sufficient to enable the railway to be reopened for traffic.

I subsequently prepared my estimates and sent them to Fred Gilbert in March 1952. The total sum amounted to £13,100. In present-day values that would be about £500,000.

Early in the New Year my work took me north to Chester and, although I received notice of a meeting to be held on April 20th 1952, I was unable to attend. I then lost touch with the London based group that was beginning to make some progress towards identifying means whereby the FR could be reopened. It was not until September 1954 that I made contact again and my first practical efforts followed in February 1955. I took two weeks holiday before starting work for a new employer and divided the time between the Talyllyn and the Festiniog. I had already met and worked with Morris Jones, the old FR fitter, at Towyn, so I was welcomed at Boston Lodge. I was given the task of drilling and tapping holes in the bottom of the foundation ring of *Prince's* new boiler for the ashpan-mounting studs. I made a number of subsequent visits to Boston Lodge, partly to dismantle derelict Quarrymen's carriages for running gear parts for the Talyllyn.

Another task with which I assisted was cutting down wood keys for the track with the circular saw bench driven by the single cylinder Crossley oil engine. The keys had been made during the War for use with main-line rails and a large quantity had been obtained, probably at firewood price They required to be cut down in width to suit the smaller FR chairs. Each key was placed in a jig with a long handle to be safely presented to the saw. The resulting key and offcut were then separated and another key placed in the jig. It was quite a quick operation. However, the Crossley engine, which had a "hit and miss" governor to control its speed, was inclined to be temperamental. When the speed reached the maximum allowed, the governor lifted a bypass valve on the fuel pump. It was supposed to close again when the speed had dropped sufficiently.

Unfortunately, the bypass sometimes failed to close properly so the engine then died. The valve then had to be re-seated manually before the engine could be started again. In order to avoid this delay it was the practice to govern the engine manually by having someone to open and close the bleed screw to keep the speed just below the point where the governor operated.

Of course, the other great game with the Crossley was to get it started at all. It was of the type known as a "hot bulb" oil engine. Unlike modern diesels, which rely on the heat of compression to fire the fuel, the old low-compression engines required an additional source of heat. This took the form of a bulbous projection on the cylinder head, which was not cooled. To start the engine this bulb had to be heated red hot with a blowlamp and the engine then turned by hand preferably with three people on the handle. If heavily loaded the engine would then run hot enough to be able to dispense with the blowlamp but on light intermittent load, such as cutting keys with the saw, it sometimes required extra heat. If the bulb became too hot it caused pre-ignition and the engine would then begin to knock. By present day standards it may seem very primitive but it enabled the work to be done.

Among other incidents was the occasion when Allan asked me to run Arthur Mills home to Penrhyn on *Busta*. This was a small powered trolley, I believe something left over from the Col. Stephens era, which had been fitted with a replacement engine. All was well until we were just approaching Penrhyn when it began to slow down although the engine revs did not drop. The chain sprocket had come loose on the axle so Arthur had to walk and I returned to Boston Lodge mainly by gravity.

On one occasion one of the "Bug Box" four-wheelers was in the works and I was down in the pit. Allan called out: "While you are down there, just have a look at the brakes" to which I responded "There aren't any!"

My increasing involvement with the Talyllyn meant that I had little time to spare to help on the Festiniog although on a number of occasions I was able to assist in salvaging wagons in Minffordd yard while selecting some for use on the Talyllyn. I drove the Simplex tractor several times between Boston Lodge and Minffordd. One had to be careful not to stall the engine as it was impossible to insert and swing the starting handle where the stone walls were close to the line.

5. Wagons were abandoned not only in the station area, but on the harbour side. Tourism barely existed here in the post-war years, so it mattered not. (GFP)

6. The ruined signal gantry emphasised to all Cob road users that the FR had been abandoned. (RWFS)

(top right)
7. Moving to the other end of the Cob on 22nd July 1952, we can examine some of the coaching stock forgotten since 1939. The Boston Lodge foundry chimney is on the left. (GEB)

(right)
8. The chimney is right of centre in this depressing view from later 1954. Coaches nos. 21 and 16 are included and the hearse is nearest to the camera. (RWFS)

I reckon I have been particularly fortunate to be of an age to be still capable of coal-firing a steam locomotive and yet to have ridden regularly on the Festiniog Railway in the early 1930s during our traditional family holidays in North Wales and to remember it well in those pre-war days. Other elements in my good fortune were having a father who took a keen interest in railways and a long-suffering, understanding mother! So we rode on the Welsh Highland and the Lynton & Barnstaple as well, perhaps sensing with their closure the first cold hand of the changing order of things leading up to the war, its depredation of so many established institutions and the final collapse of the FR's financial viability. Nevertheless it is an important wedge-stone and the Festiniog had made a sufficiently deep impression on me as a schoolboy to find me nosing around Tan-y-Bwlch station during 1947.

After dinner on the Friday of Whitsuntide, 1947, we walked up from the Oakeley Arms to Tan-y-Bwlch station to see if the Railway looked as if it was still in use, and as a result of this inspection Michael Low and I visited Robert Evans in his incredible office at Portmadoc on the Monday of that same weekend, after walking to Tyler's Curve and back from Tan-y-Bwlch for a more detailed look at the rails and sleepers. Having established our bona fide interest, which was not too difficult as we were both professional railwaymen from the LMS and our visit preceded what must later have become a tiresome procession of curiosity seekers, we spent an intriguing and nostalgic day of discussion and inspection.

As might be imagined, so soon after the line had closed down, what we saw in the Works, yards and stations looked pretty good. It was the condition of the track and its reinstatement to an acceptable passenger-carrying standard which exercised our greatest concern, but we could see a future in it and our enthusiasm was fuelled by the prospect of running our own railway and so avoiding the web of nationalisation, which had now become an inescapable fate for the main line systems following the post-war tide of socialism.

Discussions followed with Mr Davies in London; and it was no small surprise to me, although perhaps a timely experience in business attitudes, to meet and negotiate with a man who virtually owned a railway, but apparently had no love or sentiment for it. I suppose having spent four years at Crewe "shops" and Leeds Holbeck Motive Power Depot in overalls alongside people mostly doing a job as a railwayman because it was their locally available means of economic survival, I should have been ready to meet up with a non-proprietorial interest at other levels in the industrial jungle. However, I thus learnt a useful lesson in the advantages of discussing business matters unemotionally.

We were not told of the approaches made to the GWR, although these must have been more or less concurrent with our visits. We did learn, however, that Mr Davies was a willing seller and was prepared to gather together a package which he was sure would be acceptable to sufficient shareholders to enable us to gain control of the Company.

It was then possible to start doing our sums. Certain basic assumptions had to be made at this preliminary stage, such as Mike and I would provide the practical skills and Boston Lodge Works would yield all the materials and tools necessary to get one train (I think we based our original plan on one loco and four coaches) into service within a year.

The track was our main concern. Not the tangle of growth that we faced seven years later, but the state of sleepers, rail and keys. We could see a year's work for a gang of three and our inspections along the route generated calculation of quantities of material needed.

More sums, and a total capital amount emerged for getting the Railway operational again. Our working capital provision was based on a full year being required for repairs and renewals to reopen a revenue-earning service, but we had both seen enough of railway operation to realise its payroll was going to be the greatest threat to achieving profitability. We proposed, therefore, in broad terms to engage only so many paid staff as were necessary to run the freight service, which in the non-tourist season would be a "one engine in steam" operation, and to man up the tourist passenger operation, requiring block-posts and intermediate stations, with volunteers who would be members of a Festiniog Railway Supporters Club. Mike and I would provide the full-time administration as well as the rolling stock maintenance resource.

Realising the importance of marketing the Railway, we had a number of schemes to attract the visitor. Many of them are now implemented, such as buffet cars (only we intended providing a full meal facility, because we were looking at a Portmadoc-to-Blaeneau line of route from the word go and had in mind a less frequent and more leisurely service). The most ambitious one has not, and is not likely to be, as it was to build a hotel at Dduallt - views, solitude, walking in the summer and skiing in the winter - which could only be reached by TRAIN!

We then approached our respective fathers for advice on how the capital sum we had estimated to be required should be raised at the lowest possible rate of interest, and this hurdle was cleared. Meanwhile we were anxiously scouring war-torn, ration-ridden Britain for sources of materials, essentially wooden sleepers and 60 lb/yd. rail. We had already got price quotations for these items, but it was a very different matter obtaining an allocation. I think the best we could do on steel at that time was about half the quantity we needed on a delivery of 18 months from the date of order, subject to Ministerial approval. This bureaucratic maze, and time, defeated us; 1st January 1948 came. Mike went to Derby as one of the youngest Assistant Works Manager appointments ever to be made and I found myself acting-assistant District Motive Power Superintendent at Rugby at the tender age of 24, shortly to go to Barrow, and then Holyhead as Shedmaster which was always considered the most favoured springboard for an LMS motive power career. My father died early in 1948 and by Easter we had decided to withdraw formally from the attempt. In retrospect, as the memory fades, I sometimes feel we may have overestimated the difficulties of obtaining materials, but timing was crucial to the financial success of our plan and as far as I can now recall it took us a good six months to become informed of the many controls and restrictions we would face in attempting to get allocations, without even starting the process of being granted them, least of all getting delivery of essential materials.

And that was that, for nearly four years. Very full years, nonetheless, with all my spare time being taken up with hill climbing and a beautiful 1929 3-litre Sunbeam which had come my way in 1950; and a new career in an international oil company and an active involvement in the Territorials.

It was early in 1952 that I received a brief note from my friend Michael Low to ask if I'd seen the insertion in the Railway Gazette advertising a meeting to be held in the Stephenson Locomotive Society rooms in London, the purpose of which was to form a Festiniog Railway preservation committee, and that he (Michael Low) had written to Mr Gilbert, whose name was given as the person calling the meeting, to say I might attend and if I did would make a good committee member.

It was a cold, grey day I remember, and the surroundings were uninspiring. I had really just gone along to listen and learn how these people had managed to get over all the hurdles that baulked Mike and me four years previously. It was with dismay that as the meeting proceeded, what I heard clearly indicated that they had not really begun to identify them. There was more talk about timetables and uniform than the realities of reinstatement of a derelict railway in financial difficulties.

Mr Gilbert (his Christian name was Fred, and I was privileged to use it as a result of making several journeys in his company to Wales in our respective motor cars - he had a much-prized Standard Vanguard, then as now acknowledged as one of the better immediate post-war models) was leading the meeting and in due course got around to the business of panning out a committee from the 25 or so people present. There is no question in my store of memories that Fred Gilbert was the prime mover and inspiration of any co-ordinated action in the calling of this meeting, its outcome and the conduct of the Society's administrative affairs through the lean years leading up to June 1954. His part in laying the hard-core cannot be overestimated. A bottle of milk raised to his lips with trembling hand was his only concession to the strain of giving his all to those early, frustrating days.

The committee, having been nominated and elected, then set about electing its officers. Gilbert's solicitor and aide-de-camp in this affair with the FR was Mr. Taylor Harris and without hesitation, in view of his preparedness to act as our legal adviser free gratis, he was voted Chairman. The only other person I knew I proposed for the committee: this was Allan Garraway (and I'd only met him twice in a BR business context). He proposed me for Vice-Chairman: and as Taylor Harris never attended any of our committee meetings until the one when we formed the Society Limited in 1954, I had an admirable apprenticeship as a chairman!

This is no disparagement of Taylor Harris; he stated from the outset he would not play an active part in our railway affairs other than to advise us on matters of company law as and when we needed it, and that he did full well when called on as we unravelled the ownership tangle of the statutory FR Company and particularly when we found ourselves in negotiations with another very competent lawyer, who at age 35 was already the Secretary and a Director of the Rootes Group, at that time probably the second most successful and influential motor car manufacturer in the country, and who also had no previous enthusiasm or sentiment for railways, called John Routly.

In those two years between forming the committee and finding the way forward to rescue the Railway, we met on a monthly routine; and as Taylor Harris left all the business of the Society and its meetings to me it was a period of some strain, the committee being a strange contrast of the starry-eyed and prophets of doom, but remorselessly with the aid of the tireless researching of Fred Gilbert we built up the acquisition jigsaw, at the same time laying the foundations for Society membership.

Bit by bit it was accepted by the committee, perhaps for me a subconscious carry-over of the 1947 synthesis, that we should need a financial backer to provide the necessary injection of initial capital to buy out the owners. We were reckoning on a quick build-up of the supporting society after acquisition sufficient to provide the working capital in terms of cash and labour to get a revenue-earning service in operation. So it was that, after a number of false hopes, we were introduced to Alan Pegler. He became something of a mystery man because we only ever saw his lieutenants, Les Smith and Trevor Bailey. It was Alan's father from whom I received the cheque (after taking tea with Mr and Mrs Pegler Senior in their luxury hotel suite overlooking Hyde Park and apparently satisfactorily passing their examination) which enabled control to change hands.

Then all the subsequent detail negotiations were thrashed out between Taylor Harris, John Routly and in the initial stages Fred Gilbert, who soon withdrew because he could not establish a working rapport with John and me. At first I found myself in the same difficulties as Fred Gilbert until I gave as good or (as bad) as I got and then made businesslike progress.

The final committee-room problem of this era was to reach a consensus that we should proceed with our negotiations with the Pegler camp knowing that at the end we, the Society, would not have an asset stake in the Company. The Society committee, after many hours of debate on this issue of inevitability, finally came round to the partnership compromise which was in due course documented as the Agreement between the two parties (printed in FR Magazine No. 51).

Although this decision to back the Pegler "marriage" was held by a comfortable majority on the committee, there was the dissident voice of Mr Nelson (whose Christian name I can't recall ever being used) and I, as Chairman of the first General Meeting held by the Society in the elegant old Portmadoc Town Hall, put the proposal to the members in 1955 only to find the committee's publicity attacked from within, by him.

Undoubtedly the acid eloquence of Mr Nelson in his call for independence and thus rejection of the Pegler package struck some sympathetic ears amongst the meeting and so we went through a rough-and-tumble of motions, counter motions, amendments and so on the like of which the Society seldom suffered again.

But the position was held. We began to build on trust and I was selected to serve on the New Company Board as (a) watchdog for the Society and (b) functional Director responsible for all Engineering matters other than Civil. In the latter capacity I negotiated the coal contracts, the repair of *Taliesin (Livingston Thompson)* by Vulcan Foundry, the B privilege travel facility for our paid staff, and so on. John Routly was for some time unconvinced that the motley of the Society were entirely suitable as a business partner, but piece by piece Alan Pegler encouraged the important role we had to play and persuaded John to allow the Society a token shareholding and yielded to the Society pressure for all remaining Pegler FR shares to be protected by Trust status.

Well - that is that! We'd launched the hull of the ship.

9. This view of the top yard also includes the landmark chimney. Palmerston is visible in the background. (RWFS)

10. Boston Lodge Works is in the background in this photograph of stock abandoned outside the locomotive shed. (RWFS)

11. Proceeding past the locomotive shed, walkers would encounter the long-disused locomotive turntable. The honorary caretaker lived in the furthest of the railway cottages in the background of this 1952 picture. (AGWG)

12. The shelter at Minffordd on the down platform was beyond repair at the time of acquisition. It was soon demolished. (RWFS)

13. The up side was recorded in 1952. On the left is the ticket office window and attendant screen. Penrhyn and Tan-y-Bwlch can be seen in pictures 66-67 and 73-74. *(RWFS)*

14. Above Tan-y-Bwlch in 1952, the route was passable, but seriously waterlogged. The present Campbell's Platform is beyond the water tank. *(AGWG)*

❧ Keith Catchpole ❧

It was clear that the FR urgently needed much unskilled labour and so I recruited boys from among my pupils at the Chace School in Enfield. They soon became known as "Tadpoles".

Trips began in the Spring of 1955, the main task being clearance of vegetation, on and around the line. I would convey three lads in my Austin 7 and a colleague would take six in his Hillman Minx. Neither vehicles were in their prime, both dating from the 1930s.

After the initial season in 1955 when trains ran from Portmadoc to Boston Lodge and back for the sum of one shilling return, thoughts were turned to repairing the track for a possible opening to Minffordd in 1956. Dense brambles were the problem in many areas, in general caused by the complete blockage of drainage. The other main problem was lack of finance.

We were surrounded by valuable scrap of all descriptions and if this asset could be realised some vital cash would be available. In the quarries and all over the Blaenau area there were a great many slate wagons (both 3 and 2 tonners) and a determined effort was now made to retrieve as many of these as possible before the line was cut ready for the new Pumped Storage scheme. I went five times - once with Allan Garraway, once with Ian Smart and three times on my own. The train formation was always the same, Simplex and coach no. 10. We dare not risk either of the main train carriages, as they would have been badly damaged when the very overgrown sections were encountered; also no. 10 had a broken headstock and only two compartments although it had a very useful large van compartment.

Departure from Port was always early, about 8am. On board was my wife, the first of the "Tadpole" contingent, first aid equipment, tools of every description, stout ropes and a primus stove plus tea brewing equipment. On Simplex was plenty of fuel, several drums of sand, two rerailing jacks and a complete set of tools. As far as Penrhyn, the going was fairly straightforward. Penrhyn level crossing usually needed tar to be removed from the rail grooves as the local council kept on filling them in. Then we ran onwards to Cei Mawr with only bramble hindrance to cope with. Once over the great embankment, the battle started.

With all the drains hopelessly blocked, water ran freely along the cuttings, the added sheep droppings forming the perfect medium for rapid growth. As one entered the rhododendron area, the line was only just passable. If we reached Tyler's cutting by 10am, we were doing well, as beyond here the going became really bad. At Tyler's, the foliage grew completely over the top, forming a partial 'tunnel' and, at Penrhediad, a complete tunnel of foliage was met.

At Tan-y-Bwlch, the Jones' usually came out to see us and a tea break was taken. Simplex would need radiator water and a general examination. Onwards, above the tree line, through the short tunnel and a pause at Coed-y-Bleddiau to say 'hello' to the Johnsons and any goats that might be around. A reasonable stretch followed on to Dduallt and soon the dreaded Moelwyn Tunnel came in sight. There is no doubt that had the Pumped Storage scheme not been built, we would never have been allowed to run through this tunnel, owing to such limited clearances. We had to risk it, although all three air shafts had loose and, periodically, dangerous rocks falling onto the track below.

Once through we traversed the desolate dry valley into Tanygrisiau station, which was still let and inhabited. From there to the road crossing at Blaenau, the way was reasonably clear and arrival time at the station was usually about midday. Our wagons were in both the former GWR and LMS yards and we had to move them ourselves mainly by hand - hard work! Sometimes the local narrow gauge shunter would round up some wagons for us and propel them on to Simplex, if we were lucky. Next came oiling the wagons, which had not turned a wheel in many a year and, where couplings were missing, we used rope. We usually left just as dusk was approaching wondering if we would make it to Minffordd. Once back at Minffordd. usually at about nine or ten in the evening, we would leave the waggons in the station. Next day they were taken down to the yard for cutting up to begin.

I became honorary Company lecturer in 1955 - the post has brought me great pleasure for over 50 years.

15. *Seen from the south in May 1952, Dduallt was a desolate location. The solitary house is obscured by the tree on the left. (AGWG)*

16. *Moelwyn Tunnel was sinister and frightening to some young explorers. The wrecked wagon and sheep skeletons at the south end added to the grim ambiance. (KC)*

ᐧᐧ Eric Cooper ᐧᐧ

In the early 1950s my interest in narrow-gauge railways was spurred on by Charles Lee's book on *North Wales Narrow Gauge Railways*, James Boyd's inspirational work *Narrow Gauge Rails to Portmadoc* and, of course, the work being done at Towyn.

The closure of my local line, the Ashover Light, occasioned much gloom; the mineral line from Crich to Bullbridge near Ambergate was close to expiring, so it was time to visit pastures new, broaden one's outlook, or whatever. Aware that matters regarding the FR revival were progressing, a fact-finding trip seemed to be the next move, so in late September 1954 I set off by road for Port. I spent a little time at Welshpool and Towyn en route, arriving at Harbour Station in late afternoon.

Depression set in. Scattered around the tracks were the remains of cut-up slate wagons and, worse, a locomotive, and my reaction was that I was too late and the scrappies had taken over.

I went along through the town and checked in at the Queen's Hotel which was to be my base for the next few days. I was greatly encouraged during the evening to learn that all was not lost and that positive things were happening as well.

Back to the Harbour Station next morning. There was no sign of anyone so I set off on foot across the Cob. Arriving at Boston Lodge, I found the place unlocked and went in expecting to find someone but no, the place was deserted, as were the adjacent houses. The upshot was that I was able to spend several hours in the area, including the running shed, marvelling at the extent of the Railway's facilities and the quantity and variety of equipment, though somewhat elderly.

It was evident that the Simplex had seen recent use, if only to tow rolling stock across the Cob to Harbour Station for scrapping, and I soon deduced from other remains in the yard that the locomotive parts I had seen at Harbour Station were those of *Moel Tryfan*. Oh dear!

My hike to Boston Lodge had been most pleasant; sunshine and glorious views up the Glaslyn estuary to the mountainous background dominated by Snowdon. The return trek could hardly have been more different: driving rain off the bay resulted in very drenched guest arriving at the Queen's, whose proprietor rose to the occasion. After a quick change, my soggy clothes were taken off to the hotel's boiler room and, the weather having changed right round again, I set off to explore the town's narrow gauge network. It was fascinating: I was becoming hooked. A somewhat non-temperance evening in the company of friendly types from the local ex-GWR loco shed (Dukedogs and Collett 0-6-0s) rounded the day off nicely.

Exploration continued next day with visits to Minffordd Station and Yard, then Penrhyndeudraeth and a track walk to a point beyond the Cei Mawr embankment where the jungle was almost impenetrable. Returning to my car, carefully re-negotiating "bedstead crossing", of which more later, I set off for Tan-y-Bwlch.

Today, it is difficult to recall my impressions of TyB in 1954. It seemed almost a frontier between the dense woodland below and the bleak moorland toward Blaenau. So I continued onwards and upwards and eventually reached the Moelwyn Tunnel entrance. I decided not to explore its exceedingly damp interior and followed the original route. Just short of Tanygrisiau I decided to leave the rest for the morrow and set off back to TyB. The weather had been most kind; it had been a most interesting and exhilarating walk, but I hardly saw a soul.

Next day I had a good old root round Blaenau, which at that time was full of railway interest, before setting off on the lonely road to Bala and home. A point of interest after Llangollen (actually Froncysyllte) was to cross a narrow gauge line, itself crossing the A5 on the level, and seeing a horse-drawn train of wagons, presumably waiting to cross. It must have come from the nearby canal wharf. I waited a little while until it became obvious that the highway crossing was not imminent.

Soon after that visit, a letter came from Allan Garraway advising me that working parties were starting almost immediately and recommending the Commercial Hotel. Arrangements were speedily made and it is with pleasure that I recall the many happy times I stayed there. The Owen family made everyone welcome and I am sure they contributed greatly to the success of the working parties.

I decided to try travelling by train but I only ever did it once. The trip involved changes at Derby, Crewe, Chester, Bangor and Afonwen. Not without interest in those days but very time-consuming. As the journey progressed it became apparent that one other passenger was heading in the same direction, and so I met Joe Rivett from Manchester, who was also staying at the Commercial.

Next day I found myself attached to a small group engaged in revitalising some of the Boston Lodge machinery, in particular a very ancient Crossley diesel engine which took ages and ages, plus several people, to get started, and also a circular saw bench. This took several weekends and its main purpose seemed to be to reprofile the secondhand, ex-BR bull-head rail chair keys to FR size. This was a job not without its perils!

Most people went off line-clearing in those days but I always seemed to be kept busy around Boston Lodge, which was ideal on wet days. There was plenty going on, with work on the rebuilding of *Prince* and the inspection, repair and painting of coaches.

One interesting job was to convert the Simplex to run on TVO (tractor vapourising oil). The Dorman engine drank petrol at the rate of two miles per gallon, sometimes worse, and petrol cost the then ruinous price of four shillings (20p) a gallon, so something had to be done. It was decided to copy a farm tractor system in which the engine was started on petrol and, when warm, switched over to run on TVO. It had been noted that during operation the Simplex exhaust pipe at the manifold end ran red-hot. So the TVO line from its tank was coiled around the pipe a couple of times on its way to the changeover tap en route to the carburettor. This appeared to do the necessary, well most of the time, and as TVO only cost nine pence (4p) a gallon, there was an obvious benefit. At a later date the Dorman was replaced by a diesel engine but this was after my time.

I recall arriving one time to find a catastrophe in the way of a fracture in the main shaft of the Simplex. Unbelievably, a spare gearbox appeared, "liberated" I believe from a similar loco which it just so happend had been abandoned after the lifting of the Croesor Tramway section of the Welsh Highland. So one day's work for three of us was to remove the old box, install the "new" unit and have a trial trip. This was actually achieved on a one-day trip from the Derby area.

One day a gentleman named Ian Smart, well known among the fraternity, rolled up with an intriguing load on his trailer. This appeared to be a combination of a small petrol engine, a motorcycle gearbox and what could have been a platelayer's trolley. Most importantly, it went. After a few test runs, a small flat-wagon was attached, some five or six of us scrambled on board and off we went up the line. I seem to recall a minor derailment just before Penrhyn where some rocks had been washed onto the track. The barrier at "Bedstead Crossing" was carefully dismantled and we carried on until the clutch started to slip. After load reduction (read: "Get off you lot at the back") the motive power proceeded on its way . The "reduced load" portion decided to press on anyway on foot and we all met up at Tan-y-Bwlch where we enjoyed a chat with the Jones Family.

Eventually, as it was getting dark, we all set off for Boston Lodge and, as of course it was all downhill, there was no recurrence of the clutch problem. It really was quite pleasant; the engine chuntering away, the clicks of the wheels on the rail joints, until a sudden call from the front: "Look out there's a ..." followed by a crashing noise and then another. We came to a halt to discover that, while we had been up the line, the user of the crossing had re-assembled his museum pieces across the track. It may have been this incident that inspired the name *Busta* for Ian's masterpiece.

More seriously, considerable efforts were being put into the re-building of *Prince*, refurbishing coaches, fettling up the track around the Harbour Station and the station building itself as the projected re-opening day (expected to be late July) drew ever closer.

I arrived for my summer "holiday" just after the opening day and was immediately pressed into service as train driver, using the Simplex and the two coaches which had been restored. The service ran across the Cob to just beyond the old running shed where there was good public access.

There was no run-round facility, so it was necessary to propel the empty stock down to the Works entrance, where we stopped short of the points; the coaches were then uncoupled, pushed by hand through the points and then set back into the Yard, whereupon the Simplex collected them and propelled them back up to the waiting passengers, and so back to Port. The operation was not without its hazards, but we all survived. What was most encouraging was the keen level of interest and ridership.

There was a curious incident one day. I felt a slight jolt on the loco at one point which markedly increased the next time. After coupling off at Harbour Station I ran the loco back to the location for a look-see and discovered that a short length of the rail web had disintegrated due to corrosion, and the running surface now had a pronounced dip, hence the jolt. A nice job for the back shift to change the rail for the next day. It should be remembered that the Cob track had not been used for many years as the slate traffic had terminated at Minffordd Yard. The Cardigan Bay weather had taken its toll.

At some point on my sixth day of duty, *Prince*, having been completed and tested, took over the service and I started looking round for another project. This was to come sooner than I expected. Meantime ...

"The realisation of redundant assets". This bit of modern jargon refers to an interesting day spent by four of us in Minffordd Yard dragging slate wagons out of bushes which had grown around them, using the Simplex and marshalling them into a train in the station loop. We managed to rescue 28 of them, if my memory is correct, and it made quite an impressive sight as, together with a brake van, we headed to Boston Lodge where they were parked pending disposal.

There was concern that the only stand-by motive power was the elderly Simplex, so thoughts turned to investigating the potential of the "equally elderly" Baldwin petrol engined loco lurking at the back of the shed. After approval from on-high, the loco was hauled down to the Works for appraisal. Such information as we had suggested that the loco had always been unreliable and lacking in power. The sump contained a substance which I would hesitate to call lubricating oil. It was more like tar and most unsuitable for a splash-feed system, so it was changed. The fuel system was flushed out, the spark plugs cleaned and we found, surprise, surprise, that the magneto worked. Now to start it! The cranking handle was a fearsome thing, about five feet long, inserted from the rear of the cab. After many, many turns, and a few coughs (from the engine) it was decided to try tow-starting. This did the job but the clanking noises from the engine were ominous. The engine was removed and stripped down. It was considered to be of museum quality only. The obvious solution would be a replacement power unit, especially as the rest of the loco seemed rugged and serviceable. I knew of a 2-cylinder Gardner diesel engine lying out-of-use in a haulier's garage and, after some haggling, he agreed to sell it for £25. Now to convince the FR; money was still very tight. Approval came, plus a note from Allan Garraway, to get it installed ASAP.

It was stripped down locally (Duffield, Derbyshire), cleaned, components such as valves, injectors and fuel pump overhauled and, courtesy of Ian Smart and HUN 1, transported to Boston Lodge. There the task of reassembly and installation into the Baldwin began. Quite a few people helped with the project, some without knowing, but mostly Messrs Hughes, Bett, Carr and Rusbridger of the "Derby Gang". The engine was nose-suspended and part was missing, but Fred Boughey came to the rescue with a specially carved block of wood which was just the job. Transmission from engine to gearbox was a hybrid affair gleaned from a bus (don't ask) but everything went together quite well.

Eventually the big day came. The great cranking handle (no self-starter) was inserted; a couple of pulls and the engine fired and quickly settled down to a steady rhythm. After a few movements up and down the Yard, a short trial trip on the main line proved that all was well. All very satisfying!

17. After passing through the small bore, devoid of refuges, one emerged at Tunnel Cottage, a lonely outpost. On the left of this July 1950 panorama is Brookes Granite Quarry, while, on the right, is the spoil of the zinc mine. (AMD)

18. Tanygrisiau station was inhabited during the closure period and had an unofficial external light. Only the goods shed (left) remains today. (RJ)

19. *A closer look at the shed in about 1952 includes the usual threat of prosecution, plus the less common risk of death by falling slates. (RJ)*

20. *A view down the line between the two BR stations at Blaenau Ffestiniog has the LMR one (Stesion Fein) in the distance. The offset track prevented quarry traffic between the stations leaving that route. (RWFS)*

FESTINIOG RAILWAY COMPANY

TRAIN SERVICE

PORTMADOC (Harbour) and BOSTON LODGE (for Port Meirion).

PORTMADOC Dep.

10.30,   11.30 a.m.,   1.30,   2.30,   3.30,   4.30,   5.30 p.m.

BOSTON LODGE Dep.

11.00 a.m.,   12 noon,   3.00,   4.00,   5.00,   6.00 p.m.

X. Runs when required.

FARE 1/- Return. 8d. Single.

(CHILDREN UNDER 14 HALF PRICE).

The Festiniog Railway was the prototype of narrow gauge railways throughout the world. It was opened in 1836, and steam traction was introduced in 1863, with the locomotives "PRINCE" and "PRINCESS." The passenger Service was suspended in 1939 and the line closed in 1946.

The control of the shares of the Company was obtained by a railway enthusiast in 1954, and a new Board of Directors formed. Railway enthusiasts are supporting the Railway Company financially through the Festiniog Railway Society, and nearly all the work done in restoring the line has been done by voluntary effort. Your patronage and support will aid the railway to reopen further stretches through glorious scenery, in following years.

The original locomotive "PRINCE" has been reconditioned and is once more hauling trains.

A. G. W. GARRAWAY, Manager.

❧ Roy Cunningham ❧

By the time I first became involved all the necessary and toilsome preliminaries had been concluded. The various approaches to FR Company Chairman Walter Cradoc Davies, the rescue of the Talyllyn following the death of Sir Haydn Jones, the Bristol meeting and all the subsequent activities that culminated in Alan P. obtaining control in June 1954 were already in the past. The names of all those involved are on record and they have to be admired for their courage in plunging into the unknown by undertaking the restoration of two railways for which there was no sound business case for so doing, and for planning to do it with a mix of paid and voluntary labour.

I had already seen and travelled on the Talyllyn in August 1953, then in its third year as the world's only "preserved" railway, but its magic failed to capture me and I escaped to become involved in the FR revival. About 18 months later I was one of a small group of friends who took part in a weekend working visit to the FR. We arrived in Portmadoc by train early one Saturday morning and walked into the Commercial Hotel to be greeted by Allan Garraway, then still a weekend volunteer. Robert Evans was still in post as Manager, but Allan was controlling all the restoration work.

Our task that weekend, and mine for a couple of others during the Spring of 1955, was to assist with getting carriages 12 (brake/third) and 23 (the former Welsh Highland carriage transferred to FR ownership, along with *Moel Tryfan* as "compensation" for losses sustained by the FR in operating the WHR from 1934 to 1937) ready for the first passenger service in July. One other piece of coaching stock which was in basic running order was number 10 van and this was the vehicle used for the occasional Simplex hauled Saturday evening forays up the line. The objective was to make the whole line passable, so that the large stock of slate waggons still at the top end of the line could be recovered before the track was blocked by the pumped storage works. I remember at least two trips, one of which suffered a derailment of Simplex (it spread the track) just above Penrhyn Crossing, but nevertheless reached Tan-y-Bwlch and another where we met the "wrong type of vegetation" around Rhiw Goch and were only able to progress after the "support" crew had bailed out and applied their shoulders to the rear of the train. Once moving again we had no problem in scrambling back on board no. 10's rear balcony as full speed was only around 4mph! This was the "Tan-y-Bwlch or bust!" era.

By the summer of 1955, I was becoming frustrated in that the only way I could reach the railway at weekends from the south-east was by overnight train journeys in both directions, with the return on Sunday evening involving two bus rides as far as Bangor before I could join a train. It was Allan who suggested that I should contact Leonard Heath-Humphrys to explore the possibilities of forming a group to arrange communal transport from the London area. I believe that when I made contact with Leonard he had already been in touch with one or two other like minds and on December 1st the inaugual meeting of the London Area Group of the Festiniog Railway Society was held at the now demolished Ship Tavern, just outside Liverpool Street Station. LAG letter No. ONE, the predecessor of LINK appeared in the following January, produced by Leonard in a very light hearted style, although he scrupulously obeyed the then current convention of referring to individuals by their formal titles, e.g. the treasurer was Mr Warren Jenkins and the travel officer Mr D Guard Day (although, of course, in conversation we always called them Warren and Derek respectively). Other regional groups were formed at about the same time and I am sure for very similar reasons, and for many years they were an important facet of the Society's operations.

Pioneering days, indeed. OK, I know that our friends down the coast had been operating the Talyllyn from 1951 with voluntary labour support and one could argue that they were the true trail blazers, but let us also remember one man without whose activities the restoration of the FR would have been even more difficult. If one ignores Jack Howey's young blades down on the Romney Hythe & Dymchurch Railway in the years between the wars, it was the late Rev. J Timothy (Timmy) Phillips who became the first railway preservation volunteer with his heroic and mainly successful efforts to keep the works off limits to intruders during the closure years. And, of course, some of his handiwork is still visible from the train.

21. Here is the end of the WR line from Bala, plus the FR tracks used by the local quarries. This and the previous view are from September 1954. (RWFS)

22. Turning round and going back three years, we see the ex-GWR station and goods shed. The shine on the rails shows the limit of regular shunting activities. (AMD)

*23. We end our sequence of pre-restoration photographs with this record of Robert Evans alongside **Palmerston** in March 1954. The location is seen in picture 9. (JBS)*

24. Our journey in the revival period begins in September 1954 near the extremity of the FR in Portmadoc close to the flour mill. Behind the camera is the connection to the Welsh Highland Railway; part of the gasworks is in the distance. (RWFS)

⤝ Michael Davies ⤜

My first news of the sad demise of the FR came from the *Railway Magazine* in the 'Notes & News' column of the Nov/Dec 1946 issue. Here we read "Festiniog Railway. All traffic has been suspended, although the Company assures us that it is by no means certain that this connotes abandonment, as many negotiations are in progress. The last trains for the time being ran on August 2nd, and no more than a skeleton staff has been retained". I took heart from the statement that the last trains had run 'for the time being' and a skeleton staff had been retained. Little did I know that this consisted of the elderly Robert Evans at Harbour and Morris Jones at Boston Lodge. A few months later the magazine *Railways* had a most informative article by Robin Butterell, in which he paints an extremely gloomy portrait of the railway which he visited on a very wet November day in 1946, when Morris Jones was still at Boston Lodge to show him round.

Our family holiday in 1947 was at Morfa Nevin and I was invited by the parents of another boy staying at our boarding house to join them for a trip to Barmouth in their car. The journey is still fresh in my memory for this was my first visit to Portmadoc, June 22nd 1947. My first view was of the Moel y Gest Incline as we approached from Criccieth and then, as we traversed the High Street, I saw the WHR connecting line crossing the road on to the Britannia Bridge. A line of slate wagons stood on the Oakeley Wharf, there was the briefest glimpse of Harbour Station, and then we descended out of its view on to the Cob. Great was my excitement as we approached the Toll Gate with the Boston Lodge chimney so clearly in view, but my companions were really total strangers and had no conception of the feelings of their thirteen year old passenger! Our return journey was via Rhyd, passing Tan-y-Bwlch station, and so once again I had a brief tantalising view of the railway bridge but further investigation had to wait another year.

At fourteen years of age I was thoroughly hooked, indeed my parents thought obsessed, by the Festiniog Railway and my dear aunt Dilys sportingly agreed to take me to stay with friends in Blaenau Festiniog for a few days in August 1948. The journey from Birkenhead is still very vivid in my memory. We took the Crosville "Caernarvon Express" service to Betws-y-Coed travelling on one of their pre-war Leyland 'Tiger' coaches.

We only stayed in the town for four nights but it felt like weeks. My bedroom in Glan-y-Pwll road faced straight up the Nidd-y-Gigfran incline, and I could relate to this by studying the photograph in Lee's book, which I now know to be one of Bleasdale's official photos taken in 1887. Our host, Mr Pritchard, worked at Llechwedd, and we eagerly accepted his offer to conduct us over the quarry during our stay. This was indeed a memorable visit and perhaps the highlight was when we entered the dressing mill to watch the slates being cut.

On another day I persuaded auntie that we must visit Tan-y-Bwlch. The very steep gradient to the station severely taxed her and she was very glad to sit down on an abandoned wagon in the siding before we set off for Dduallt. We spoke to Mrs Bessie Jones and I recollect auntie enquiring if any eggs could be purchased as we observed many hens rooting around the grass covered rails. It was well that there were none to spare as we had a very hairy descent back to the bus at Pont Tal-y-Bont. Garnedd tunnel presented no problems and we had a break at Coed y Bleiddiau before going on to Tank curve. Somewhere beyond Plas Dduallt auntie decided she had walked far enough along the railway and we agreed to seek a path down into the valley. This proved disastrous and we slipped and slithered down some precipitous rocks and were very glad indeed when we reached the old road near Dol-y-Moch. A friendly Crosville bus soon appeared to take us back up the long hill to Llan Ffestiniog and Blaenau.

On our last evening Mr Pritchard suggested I might like to accompany him and walk all the way from Glan-y-Pwll to Tan-y-Bwlch along the railway. What an offer! This was of course the highlight of the holiday and was a walk I'll never forget. No train had run for two years, but the section from Tan-y-Grisiau to Dduallt station saw regular use, albeit unofficial, by the local inhabitants. Many greetings in Welsh took place in that first mile or so as quite a few properties were still occupied in that rather bleak valley approaching the Tunnel. The tunnel keepers cottage was still inhabited and a Post Office letter box existed in the wall. Our walk through the tunnel was exciting as water cascaded down the three air shafts whilst we walked on the rail tops one arm over the others shoulder, quarry fashion. I was warned against touching the walls which were encrusted in more than eighty years of soot! At Dduallt the station house, Rhosllyn, was occupied by an elderly lady living alone, who I was told pushed the small flat bogie all the way to Tan-y-Grisiau for her shopping every week. Presumably she was able to free wheel back although I don't recollect a brake! We were now on familiar ground and Mr Pritchard told me we could have followed the well defined path from Dduallt to Rhyd Sarn if we had only continued on the track for another few minutes on our walk the previous day. Coed-y-Bleiddiau presented a rather forlorn appearance with the door open and spent candles on a solitary table. Little did I know then of it's remarkable pre-war tenant, the traitor William Joyce (Lord HawHaw) who followed on from the tenancy of the composer Sir Granville Bantock. Our memorable walk concluded, we exchanged greetings with Will and Bessie, and walked down to the Oakeley Arms for the Blaenau bus.

In October 1948 I accompanied a school friend on a five day cycle tour of Snowdonia staying at Youth Hostels.

The road to Ffestiniog was at this period little more than a mountain track beyond Capel Celyn with a grass strip down the middle, and we had to open and close gates several times. After this rather bleak moorland I felt much elation as we free wheeled down into the Vale of Ffestiniog, and at last I could go exactly where I wanted as John was very tolerant of my obsession with the FR. Boston Lodge was a 'must' and here we were able to observe carriage stock in the 'Long' shed through the broken windows. The place was then still reasonably secure as I have no recollection of 'breaking in' to which I must admit a couple of years later!

The summer of 1949 was notable for the publication of a new book entirely devoted to Snowdonia's narrow gauge railways, and for my fifteenth birthday my aunt bought me a copy of *Narrow Gauge Rails to Portmadoc* by J.I.C.Boyd. The cover price was 17/6d, quite expensive in the forties, but that book became my bible, and told me very much more than I could absorb from Lee's book in 1945.

Whilst planning our eight day cycle tour of North Wales in June 1949 I decided to write to the Mr Jones whom Butterell had met at Boston Lodge in 1946, seeking his permission to inspect the works and running shed. We now know of course that Morris Jones was paid off in the early spring of 1947, and so the reply duly came from Robert Evans at Harbour. It would appear that by now Evans was well used to such enquiries, and his letter to me was not at all what I wanted to read. 'Owing to the serious damage done to the Company's property at our Boston Lodge Works by Souvenir hunters and others, we have had to lock the works up, with the keys at this office and the place is now under Police protection, who have instruction to prosecute any person found trespassing on the premises. Under the circumstances I regret being unable to allow you to visit the works as desired' Having no desire to find ourselves under arrest, we resisted the temptation to climb into the works through one of the many missing windows and contented ourselves with walking the track and inspecting the ever more derelict stations. Back home, I realised from the preface that the writer of my latest book lived not a mile away at Brooklands, Cheshire, and so one evening in July 1949 I had the temerity to cycle round and introduce myself.

He was very tolerant, and invited me to his study where I was spell bound at the array of narrow gauge photographs and lovely models of FR rolling stock. An England engine named *Boston Lodge* was coupled to passenger brake third No 2. Excitement indeed! I was in some way able to repay his kindness by reintroducing him to a locomotive which had run on his prep school miniature railway before the war, and was now in the possession of a friend not far away near Macclesfield.

In the autumn of 1949 James Boyd gave me exciting news relating to a take over bid he and some friends were hoping to make for control of the FR, and at once the dark clouds seemed to lift and for a few months I was full of optimism for the future of my favourite railway. With hind sight it was something of a roller coaster, for at one meeting he would be full of plans for rehabilitation, and then my hopes would be dashed on the next visit by total lack of progress. In the early months of 1950 his optimism must have returned as he asked me if I would be prepared to help in a voluntary capacity on the line during the Easter school holiday, and whilst this never came to pass of course, I think I can certainly claim to be the first person ever to be asked to help run a railway without pay!

With knowledge acquired over the years since 1950, it is not difficult to see the almost insurmountable problems of those seeking to take control of the company. Boyd had a backer in the N.E. of England who was prepared to risk a few thousand pounds but this was never going to match the price the scrap men were offering. It will be recalled that the Company wcrc refused an Abandonment Order in 1951, after which time they had to agree to a lower figure. I still have a few notes from 1949/50 which now make quite interesting reading. The Boyd plan in 1949 was to abandon Boston Lodge and concentrate the workshops at the Portmadoc New site, as planned in 1923.

Trains would run over the High Street and then along the Gorseddau line to terminate adjacent to the BR(W) station. The majority of holiday makers were of course still travelling to Cardigan Bay by train at this time, although the cost of this work even in 1949 would surely have been crippling. A new halt was planned at Minffordd Crossing and trains would terminate at the LMS station in Blaenau. On the locomotive front, I was told that *Princess* could be made ready in a week and *Taliesin* in three weeks, whilst *Prince* could be reassembled using the new boiler on hand. About four carriages were deemed fit for use with little attention other than paint. For the winter service it was envisaged that the Simplex could be used with one carriage, or a rail bus introduced using a converted ex Crosville Leyland KP2 (N Type). This class were being withdrawn by Crosville at the time. There was not much discussion regarding the track other than to state that it was serviceable with minimal repair, subject to a 15mph speed limit. A few weeks later I was told that the plan to run to the BR station was on hold, but by the summer Haydn Jones at Towyn was dead, and the Talyllyn was crying out for a saviour. We know that Mr Boyd transferred his energies to the less demanding railway further south, and the FR had to wait another four years before rescue was effected.

I continued to visit the railway at every opportunity during the early 1950s and succeeded in walking every section other than Penrhyn to Boston Lodge which had become too overgrown. The section through the Plas Estate was becoming seriously overgrown with saplings, gorse and rhododendron, and I only just got through in February 1950, the last time until our early forays of the 'new' era in December 1954.

By the high summer of 1950 I felt less intimidated by the Evans letter, and thought it very unlikely I would be arrested by a constable of the Merioneth County Constabulary if found taking photographs inside Boston Lodge Works. I went in several times through missing windows on the rear wall, unbolting a door from the shops into the main yard, and then returning the same way! I can't remember the procedure for gaining access to the running shed, but it was all too easy by then. My only embarrassing visit was in 1953, when having broken in and set up my camera, I heard voices close by. In panic I hid in a cupboard until the voices receded, creeping out and making good my escape. I soon discovered that it was our old friend the Revd Tim Phillips taking round a couple of other enthusiasts! He later accompanied me on an 'official' tour and explained what he was doing to try and secure the premises from thieves. This he largely succeeded in doing and we must be ever grateful to him. A quiet man of great charm, I must admit to not placing much credence in his forecast that the FR would be open again within a year or so. How wrong one can be!

Another memorable incident at this period was our walk from Blaenau to Tan-y-Bwlch on the Saturday of August Bank Holiday weekend 1952. My auntie May usually spent the holiday in North Wales and agreed to accompany me on this walk. We came over the Bala & Festiniog line where I received quite a nasty burn to the eye through looking out of the carriage window. Luckily the pain subsided just as we were about to walk into the Cottage Hospital in Blaenau! Our walk was very pleasant in the warm August weather and we paused at the Tunnel to inspect the old Brookes Quarry siding. By this time the Tunnel Cottage was unoccupied. Imagine my delight at finding one of the German bogies moveable if a little stiff, and I was tempted to push it out onto the main line, working the ground frame to change the points which were set for the 'main'. This would be because the resident at Dduallt still came that way on her weekly shopping trip! Auntie seemed to enjoy the experience until some yards into the tunnel, when she was gripped by claustrophobia.

Nothing I could do would pacify her and she fled out on foot to climb over the mountain. I took the wagon through and then set off back to meet her close to one of the air shafts. We resumed the journey, and there was no sign of life at Dduallt, but on our approach to Coed y Bleiddiau I spotted the Johnson's trolley parked outside the cottage. This they used to convey their groceries up from Tan-y-Bwlch as there is of course no road access here and it was long before they owned a vehicle, which they later drove part way up the forest track from Tafarn Trip. Not wishing to confront them, we abandoned the bogie, but I noticed later that it was parked in the siding at Tan-y-Bwlch. The only other changes noted on that August visit were yellow surveyors marks on the rails across the Cob, and a 3-ton slate wagon which had appeared on the Welsh Highland connecting line near the Britannia Bridge. Auntie lived to see the line reopened through to Blaenau, but she often recalled the Moelwyn Tunnel incident!

With my release from the Forces in September 1954, I was able once more to make regular trips to Merionethshire, and before that month was out the 'grape vine' told us that something was happening on the FR. With my friend Bob Fysh, I went to the Talyllyn AGM at Towyn on September 25th and it was here that rumour abounded. We did our usual stint on the permanent way there, but on Sunday afternoon we knocked off early and headed home by a rather devious route which encompassed Boston Lodge. Whilst all was quiet here we were not disappointed for it was at once apparent that the Simplex had been busy shunting rolling stock which had remained in the same positions the whole time I had known the Festiniog Railway.

Impatient to discover what was happening, I set off by train for North Wales on October 23rd. The rain that day just fell in solid sheets, and emerging from the two mile smoke filled tunnel, Blaenau presented a most desolate sight. My heavy army cape did nothing to prevent the rain from reducing my state to the proverbial drowned rat, and the weather was little better at Minffordd. With no sign of any changes at the station, and with the track still impenetrable below Minffordd Crossing, I trudged my sodden way by road towards Boston Lodge, only to discover later that Simplex had reached within a few yards of the crossing on October 3rd. Feeling wet and a little depressed my spirits rose on hearing what I later came to know as the Simplex sound - petrol driven then and showering sparks from her exhaust, which often glowed red. Allan Garraway and Len Heath Humphrys were busy shunting and sorting wagons and I was asked if I would assist. Wagons from Harbour were brought over to Boston Lodge shed yard for scrapping, work which occupied the rest of the daylight hours, and also depleted the petrol tank of the very thirsty Simplex. This necessitated working the tractor over the Britannia Bridge to a point near the petrol station where 16 gallons were purchased (at 4/6d per gallon!).

In the gathering dusk, clearance to drier weather encouraged us to clear the main line a little further and, so like a small tank with armour plating, we roused the echoes beneath Rhiw Plas bridge and on past the cemetery. We ran over Minffordd Crossing for a distance of ten yards, the first train for over eight years! Here a figure emerged from the gloom in the form of Robert Smallman, asking could he assist us in any way. Robert has been a personal friend now for over half a century, and has provided assistance to the railway in many varied ways. Returning in total darkness we became derailed on the badly-choked crossing, but one jack and willing assistance from a band of locals, soon had us on our way. Once again in pouring rain and with trees and bushes sweeping upon us in the blackness, it was a memorable journey, and one oft times repeated in that first winter of restoration.

The Commercial Hotel, presided over by dear old Mr and Mrs David Owen, provided us with hot baths and substantial meals at a very modest price, and such was our enthusiasm to penetrate yet further up the line that we worked a pre-breakfast turn, usually rising at 6.00am and leaving Boston Lodge with the Simplex at about 6.30 for a two hour session before breakfast. This first escapade took us only to the old facing points into Minffordd Sidings where we became yet again derailed, the point being totally invisible in the boskage!

My first weekend of work on the FR concluded about 4.00pm at Minffordd Weighhouse Crossing, where our small party spent over five hours clearing eight years accumulation of stone and compressed slate dust from the rails. The next eight hours were spent travelling back to Cheshire via Bangor, on Sunday buses and trains that averaged but 15mph!

Public transport was obviously a serious deterrent to a short working weekend at Portmadoc, and has regretfully remained so ever since, so I set about canvassing friends with FR interests, arranging for at least one to be a car owner, and so on 6th November, Fred Boughey, Bob Fysh and myself became the first volunteers to make up a working party from what were later to become the Lancashire & Cheshire and Merseyside & Deeside Groups.

6th November 1954 was something of a red letter day in FR annals, Robert Evans, Manager for nearly twenty-five years, and with over sixty years service, being presented with a handsome clock by the new directors, at a short ceremony at the Queens Hotel, Portmadoc. Before the presentation a special train was run from Minffordd to Port, conveying the directors and manager, and their guests, the first 'passenger' train since September 1939.

Our first job on this date was to assist AGWG to pack the main running line with old sleepers due to an earth slip immediately beyond Boston Lodge Crossing, and we then ran the Simplex over the Britannia Bridge for petrol, hauling some rubbish-filled slate wagons as far as Harbour Station. Returning to Boston Lodge light engine, bowsider No. 17 and brake 3rd van No. 2 were hauled up to Minffordd Crossing, where the train was divided due to severe slipping, Simplex and No. 17 continuing to Minffordd Station. Van No. 2 was collected a few minutes later, and to this day I still have a mind's eye view of Bill Broadbent, Fred Boughey and other stalwarts of that time shouldering the train over the still badly choked Weighbridge Crossing, to enable the whole train to reach Minffordd. Here the press was represented by a reporter and photographer from *Y Cymro* and Alan Pegler and his fellow directors, together with officers of the infant society and Mr and Mrs Robert Evans entrained for Portmadoc. My notes indicate that our train ran non-stop, covering the journey in 17 minutes, the bogie stock running very smoothly considering its long disuse and state of the track.

The following day was another 6.30am start at Boston Lodge, and our aim was now to attempt a thrust forward through the gorse and brambles to Penrhyn. Goods brake van No. 6, used regularly during the war years, and in fact forming part of the final train on 1st August 1946, still languished in the loco shed with *Princess* and *Merddin Emrys*, just as left on that fateful day, and so in the grey light of dawn she emerged once more, after quite a battle with several stout gorse bushes to gain entry to the shed's centre road.

Our train now consisted of Simplex, Van No. 1, and three slate wagons, and the latter were detached at Minffordd Crossing to be loaded with bushes cut down from the wall. Loco and van continued to Minffordd, and then we had the exciting experience of battling on to Penrhyn light engine, reaching the crossing just west of the station before our return to Port and breakfast. A lasting memory of this first train to Penrhyn was the surprise and amazement registering on the faces of those inhabitants awakened from their Sunday morning slumber by the very close proximity of our 1917 Simplex, which in its petrol days seemed to backfire continually!

This memorable Sunday concluded with another run to Penrhyn Station to clear a large pile of logs from the track, and an afternoon spent shunting Harbour Station to separate slate wagons from a multitude of other decrepit goods vehicles, including the horse dandy.

I made two further visits to the line before the close of 1954, the first on 4-5th December and the second two weeks later - I really had been bitten by the FR bug.

Again a further assault was made into virgin mileage, and after fitting new locks to Penrhyn gates we proceeded for half a mile towards Rhiw Goch, at which point a wall had been built along the track. Co-operation from the farmer soon had it demolished and rebuilt in its former position, which enabled us to continue towards Tan-y-Bwlch.

Our activities in an area as built up as Penrhyn hardly went unnoticed, and on our return from Port after Sunday breakfast about ten volunteers, many locals, crowded into van 6 or clung to the Simplex for the next battle with Mother Nature in the woods around Gwlyb. Here, young saplings or fallen trees impeded our progress, and nearly three hours were spent using chains attached to the Simplex, saws and axes, until we were finally forced to return to Boston Lodge in rain and darkness, disappointed that the chalked slogan on the loco "Tan-y-Bwlch or bust" remained unfulfilled.

On 18th December, Ian Smart took his firm's Albion lorry from Manchester to Boston Lodge to collect a PW trolley, later to become the infamous *Busta*, for rebuilding at his works, and I accompanied him on this trip, the first of many memorable visits with Ian over the next couple of years. Morris Jones and apprentice fitter Arwyn Morgan were now working on *Prince*, a heartening sight which augured well for the proposed 1955 reopening to passengers, and valuable publicity was being gained from the visit of a newspaper photographer from one of the national dailies.

Ian and I were detailed to go up to Tan-y-Bwlch and bring down to Penrhyn a flat wagon, clearing track en route, and we did in fact succeed in removing one fallen tree clear of the rails, and partially cutting up another. Penrhyn was reached in darkness after a very exhilarating and nerve wracking gravity run, for our wagon had no brakes! We then returned to Tan-y-Bwlch Station in a vintage Penrhyn taxi to collect the Albion left there earlier.

The early months of 1955 continued in the pioneering spirit, and each visit would see further progress towards the goal of running a train right through to Blaenau Ffestiniog Central station. On our first visit that year we spent much time in the woods clearing some sizeable trees which had fallen across the track in the years of closure, and with the return of *Busta* on January 22nd we were able to run right up and into the Moelwyn Tunnel with a small gang of volunteers travelling on a light trolley.

The Tanygrisiau Pumped Storage Scheme of the Central Electricity Authority had been much discussed in FR circles and on February 5th it was arranged that the FR directors meet CEA officials on site. To create the best effect it was decided that a train be run up to Tanygrisiau, and this consisted of the Simplex and No 1 Van. This train later succeeded in crossing Glan-y-Pwll Road and reaching 'Stesion Fein' the LNW Junction Station. A few weeks later on Saturday March 5th the whole line was finally reopened with the running of Simplex plus 'bowsider' no 17 and Van No 1. The return run of this train will forever remain with me. Leaving Blaenau in the late afternoon, Ian Smart and I sat in the first class compartment of this carriage, and we enjoyed the wonderful sensation of gliding down the old route past Doppog to the Tunnel. The riding was very smooth considering the track had not seen any maintenance, or the carriage turned a wheel since 1939. We were a little apprehensive in the tunnel as Allan appeared to hardly check the speed, and we knew there was a broken rail beneath one of the air shafts! However, we emerged into what was now almost total darkness, and continued in like manner through Tan-y-Bwlch and down to Penrhyn gates. Port was reached in little more than today's standard running time, a great achievement considering that it was only a matter of weeks since our first endeavours. Another run was made about this period for the benefit of Mr P.B.Whitehouse and friends, the train this time consisting of Third Brake No2 and the Simplex. Allan asked me to officiate as guard, my only trip in this capacity, and my recollection is of sitting in the guards ducket when a particularly large branch struck the coach side near Plas and broke the narrow window, resulting in my receiving a cut to the face! The Festiniog Railway was certainly open once more, although the loss of the section between Dduallt and Tanygrisiau early in 1957 makes the memory of these few early trips to Blaenau all the more precious.

With the re-engagement of fitter Morris Jones and his apprentice Arwyn Morgan at the start of 1955 the company was desperately looking for additional cash, and I volunteered to sell off some of the vast stock of tickets we had discovered at Harbour Station. I recall going, with some trepidation, to the home of Robert Evans one Sunday morning in January 1955 to obtain loan of the office keys. Even Allan Garraway had still to do this in those very early days! The office was like an Aladdin's cave and we estimate there was anything up to half a million tickets in drawers and cupboards, many dating back to the very early days. In the booking office everything had been left exactly as it was on the last day of passenger services, September 15th 1939 - only the Quarrymen's train ran on the final day, Saturday September 16th. The date press showed 15SEP39 and the bottom tickets in the tubes were turned upright ready for issue. In fact, this situation obtained also at Minffordd, and Tan-y-Bwlch, but at Penrhyn and Blaenau (LMS) the offices had been ransacked and the ticket stocks largely stolen. These stations it should be remembered had no custodian living on the premises, and we must be thankful to Mr & Mrs Ellis Jones at Minffordd and Will & Bessie Jones at Tan-y-Bwlch for their ever watchful presence.

At Minffordd, not only were the ticket stocks intact, but hanging from their strings were the 1939 summer timetables of both the LMS and GWR, each endorsed 'Minffordd FR' and with the relevant table number of the Coast Line and Conway Valley Line pencilled on their covers. A perfect time warp!

As we were always fully occupied working on the line during our weekend visits it was necessary to bring the tickets home for sorting and sale to collectors, and so this was an early 'homework project'. The sheer volume of varieties was daunting with over 600 types of FR and nearly 200 types of WHR. There were still large numbers of the old second class variety withdrawn on October 1st 1908, not to mention 'Police Officer on Duty' and every conceivable sort of Quarrymans/Workmans ticket. The child equivalent of the latter were endorsed 'LAD'!

Also found in one of the cupboards was the ticket cabinet from Duffws Station which had closed in 1930 and needless to say, the cabinet was still full of tickets. The FR never disposed of anything! Transporting the tickets back to my home in Cheshire was quite difficult, and on one memorable occasion I remember Allan Garraway and Bill Hoole each nursing a drawer of tickets all the way to Crewe station when Ian Smart was giving them a lift back to their London train. Ian was still finding tickets in the interstices of his car months later! The initial response from members and other collectors was overwhelming following the first announcement offering tickets for sale, and in one post alone in January 1955 I received twenty one orders to the value of £27, a not inconsiderable sum at the time, and over the following three years I raised more than £350 for the rehabilitation of the FR.

Now that we had the line open to Blaenau again the major preoccupation was to have a train ready to operate a passenger service for the summer, and some of my time was spent at Boston Lodge assisting with carriage painting, or on the Cob fettling the track. However, my most interesting task was to walk the whole line and record every wagon still existing, with its location. This was very difficult at Minffordd as many wagons were completely hidden in undergrowth on the sunken road, whilst a large number were now devoid of their painted number. The survey took me up several inclines at Blaenau, but bad weather and the complexity of quarry lines there resulted in quite a few escaping the net.

After that memorable run down from Blaenau on March 5th, the next red letter day that year was the official reopening of the railway to passenger traffic on July 23rd. The Inspecting Officer was due on the 21st and one of my treasured possessions is a Post Office telegram sent to me by Allan Garraway at 4.21pm that day. It reads 'Inspection satisfactory. Opening Saturday afternoon. Allan'. These days we are well used to road traffic jams, but in 1955 these were confined to certain black spots on high days and holidays, but it so happened that the route from Manchester to North Wales on July 23rd was in that category. I alerted Ian Smart to the news from Allan, and he agreed we should go over to travel on the opening train, but alas due to the aforesaid traffic we only just reached Boston Lodge as the first train arrived there. However, we did manage to travel on the first train back to Port, a journey that so many of us had thought an impossible dream. The next milestone of 1955 was the return to traffic of the steam locomotive *Prince* on August 3rd. My parents and sister, sharing some of my enthusiasm, had booked their annual holiday at Borth-y-Gest for late August, and I joined them there for the first week of September. My first view of a FR steam train was from the little headland at Borth as *Prince* made her way back from Boston Lodge, and the thrill of that view and the sound of her whistle will always remain with me. The following few days were spent partially in the booking office and partially accompanying the family on walks up the Gorseddau line or Cwm Croesor. I quite enjoyed the booking office, still with its typical booking window, although the ever present smell of gas (the office was still gas lit) was not so pleasant. Quite a few locals were out to renew acquaintance with their railway, and I was sometimes addressed in Welsh. Sadly we didn't use the Edmondson date press, possibly because the 10,000 tickets supplied for the reopening were not standard Edmondson cards. They were a pink card which I think were cut in half if issued to children, or for the single journey and the fare to Boston Lodge was 1/- return.

25. Harbour Station on 7th November 1954 presented an air of optimism after 15 years of dereliction. The level crossing in the foreground was still in use. (AGWG)

*26. Sale of scrap metal was vital for fund raising and the WHR 0-6-4T **Moel Tryfan** was cut up at the station. The wheels are being loaded on 23rd October 1954. (RWFS)*

27. Seen on the same day are the cylinders of the famous NWNGR single Fairlie locomotive. Some scrap was melted in the Britannia Foundry in the background. (RWFS)

28. The arm of the signal for WHR trains, seen at the end of Britannia Terrace, was permanently lowered, apt on 23rd October 1954 during this funeral pyre for elderly slate wagons. (RWFS)

❧ Phillip Vaughan Davies ❧

I paid annual visits to the Ffestiniog which was silently mouldering away and I spent many hours talking to Bessie at Tan-y-Bwlch; Will was then working for the County Council. At Porthmadog the situation was, as described by so many, most depressing with the tracks filled with rotting vehicles; Robert Evans presided over all from his office on the first floor.

Each year I visited Robert Evans and I would be received with the utmost courtesy. We reminisced long, in Welsh, over old times; he was convinced that the Railway would never run again, and in the circumstances as they seemed at the time, it was difficult not to agree with him. He took his orders from Cynan Davies, a London-based solicitor, who was the Company Secretary and one of the family of the late W.R.Davies of Pwllheli, one-time partner of Lloyd George, and Chairman of the FR from 1925-34; the family held a majority share-holding, or at least the biggest individual share-holding, and were also interested in the Snowdon Mountain Railway.

Some time during this period I visited one of the family at Pwllheli to enquire as to the prospect of re-opening; I received a very frosty reception and failed to elicit any information other than that it seemed that in the final days of running, the FR had relied heavily on payment by the GWR to bring slate to Minffordd rather than Blaenau. With the nationalisation of the railways impending, it was apparent that such inducements would not be forthcoming in the future.

On each of my visits, Evans would take me on a tour of Boston Lodge; this was a privilege as access was generally forbidden owing to theft and vandalism; he gave me a set of plans of the line and a disused token, both of which I treasure to this day.

About this time I found an opportunity, in Suffolk, to use a narrow-gauge line to re-claim an area of wet land which was distant from the nearest hard road. I bought about a mile of track and some wagons from W.O.Williams of Harlech ("Will Scrap") and my little railway proved itself very useful.

Narrow Gauge Railways to Portmadoc by J.I.C.Boyd was published about this time. This was devoured line by line and drawing by drawing. I sent him a letter of thanks and received a very nice letter in return; this was, I feel, the match that lit the fuse giving rise to the great revivals. In the 1950s we were still debilitated by the war but beginning to look round and treasure what heritage remained; Boyd and, in a different way, Heath Humphrys, persuaded disparate people that they were not the only ones concerned with this, and I shall always be grateful to them and their like.

On one of my later visits to Robert Evans, he told me that he had been instructed to give access to Boston Lodge to two "kids", one of whom had the cheek to call himself a "railway engineer"! He said they were called "Garnaway" and "Humphreys" (sic). Much later, when I met Garraway, I fully understood Evans' misconception. Garraway loooked very young; hardly one's idea of the capable engineer that he was.

In April 1954 I moved to live in Dolgellau and came to know well Tom Lloyd Jones, the local reporter for the Welsh weekly *Y Cymro*; he was a most amiable character - short, balding, with heavy horn-rimmed glasses and a formidable battery of fountain pens in his breast pocket. He was, as is almost inevitable in Wales, known by a nickname, either as "Dr Goebbels" or, more generally, as "Jones Bach Y Cymro". Early one evening in August 1954 he rang me in some excitement - did I know there was a Mr Gilbert staying at the Oakeley Arms, Maentwrog, who represented some people who were going to take over the Ffestiniog Railway? Within half an hour, Jones Bach and I were sitting in the Oakeley Arms listening to Mr Gilbert who explained the position regarding one Alan Pegler and the acquisition of the controlling interest. We were also told of, and invited to, the inspection of the line that was to be made by the Inspecting Officer of Railways on August 18th.

There is a saying in Wales on the lines of the English "February fill-dyke" which is "Llif Awst" meaning August Flood! The night of August 17th provided a rainstorm to justify the saying fully. Well prepared for the weather, we met on the morning of the 18th at Glan-y-Pwll. I consider this to be Act 1, Scene 1 of the revival. We met Colonel McMullen, Alan Pegler, Trevor Bailey,

Bill Broadbent, Heath Humphrys and of course Gilbert and we both promised to do our utmost to help. One important aspect was to get as favourable a press as we could, and certainly Jones Bach achieved this in so far as the Welsh papers were concerned. Also, in a subtle way, he got his superior, Geoff Charles, interested. He was one of the most respected photographers and press-men in Wales. He became a real enthusiast and has served the Ffestiniog very well indeed over the years.

At this meeting, Alan Pegler told me of a rumoured hydro-electric scheme and asked if I knew anything about it. I told him that I did not but I would enquire; he also told me of a letter he had received from the local MP, T.W.Jones, welcoming the efforts to re-open the line and promising every assistance he could offer. It was obvious that at the time the MP knew nothing of the hydro scheme, for he quickly changed his tune as soon as he did; years later, when he wrote his autobiography, as Lord Maelor, he listed the Tanygrisiau scheme as among the many "blessings" that he had brought to his constituency.

Colonel McMullen looked quizzically at the Barlwyd Bridge and at the PW trolley that Will Jones had pushed up from Tan-y-Bwlch and which had figured so much in pre-war photographs, trailing behind the slate wagons. We made our way, taking it in turns to ride along a sodden track, towards Tanygrisiau where the Colonel looked non-plussed for a moment and turned to me asking "What the hell happened here?" I explained to him about right-hand running, which explained what was, to him, a most unusual layout. I felt great pride, for Jones Bach and I were the only ones present who remembered the line running; this was short-lived however, for shortly after I met Dr Bailey, father of Trevor Bailey, who told us how he had travelled the line during his honeymoon several years before I was born!

It is difficult to express the immense happiness and excitement that this meeting brought to me; I did not give much thought to the difficulties that were to come, but set about gathering information about the hydro-electric scheme. I found that the British Electricity Authority (BEA), later to become the Central Electricity Generating Board (CEGB), were playing their cards very close to their chests; enquiries with local authorities and others met with evasion and often with down-right refusal to discuss details. At this stage, the BEA were loth to disclose that the Railway would be blocked and were concentrating their efforts in persuading the people of Blaenau of the paradise that would come with the scheme. It is perhaps easy to forget the harsh economic circumstances that prevailed, especially in Blaenau, where a tragically high percentage of the male population were unemployed; the coming of such a major civil engineering scheme would seem a blessing, and the BEA did their utmost to take advantage of this.

Jones Bach and I spent many hours (and sank many pints of bitter) pondering on the non-availability of plans; his local knowledge was invaluable in formulating the simple scheme which we eventually carried out, whereby I walked into certain premises, with a roll of old maps under my arm, found the repository of a set of plans of the BEA scheme and put the old maps in their place and walked out with the BEA ones. Within an hour they were on their way to London and within less than 24 hours they were back with copies that I kept. I then performed the reverse operation, replacing the BEA plans in their original repository and recovering my old maps without anyone being aware that they had been borrowed.

I spent many hours studying these plans, but the only matter which really concerned me was that the top water level proposed for the lower Llyn Ystradau would flood the tunnel and the line upwards for some distance towards the proposed power station. Exact comparison of levels with the FR plans, which dated from the 1830s, was not possible. The BEA's, as expected, were based on Ordnance Datum while the FR's plans were based on a datum on the old sluice bridge at Porthmadog, which was demolished around 1850! Gradually, as time went on, the BEA disclosed this and the impression given to the populace was that it was the Power Station OR the Railway, which in any case was totally irrelevant in that it was the toy of little boys playing with trains or that it had been acquired by wicked financial manipulators who were only interested in compensation.

This sustained and determined attempt to steam-roller the Railway Company annoyed me intensely; I was obviously much younger then and much more impetuous and my desire to see the FR running again bordered on the fanatical. I resolved that nothing should be barred in the methods I would use to secure that end. An occurence which made me even more determined was that one day I received a phone call from an official of the BEA, whom I had known for some years, during which, after conventional pleasantries, he revealed that my father had been approached by the BEA with a view to making a topographical model of another power project. This possible commission might be affected or cancelled because of my activities with the FR. In short, I was being politely warned off! My reply was totally unrepeatable. In fairness however to the BEA, I do not think that this warning was inspired by anyone other than the individual concerned on his personal and misguided initiative.

In due course I was appointed "Engineer for Ways and Works". The appointment covered many functions among which was the keeping of my ear to the ground and relaying information to Trevor Bailey, Les Smith, Bill Bellamy and later F.T.Wayne. These men I came to admire tremendously for their devotion to the good cause, their expertise and their good sense; I felt very privileged to have the opportunity to work with them.

The BEA, as part of their propoganda barrage, organised many talks on the scheme and one of their speakers was given to making remarks which went far beyond the purview of any technical or economic dissertation, such remarks being by now familiar on the theme of calculating financiers and train-playing little boys. I resolved to get a tape-recording of this gentleman's lecture and found the location of a future venue which I reconnoitred thoroughly. We did not then have the pocket tape recorders available today; all I had was a Grundig recorder, which was the size of a suitcase; I found that I could hide myself in an attic near a ventilator where I could hear all that was said in the room below. I secreted myself there before the lecture, recorded the lot and inhaled much stale tobacco smoke in the process. I waited until the building emptied and found, at first, that I could not get out, but after some thought I managed to escape into the fresh night air.

I had parked my car, for tactical reasons, some distance away and I hoped that I did not look too much like a burglar with a suitcase of loot; as I approached the car there was a policeman, whom I knew, standing near it; he greeted me in a friendly fashion in Welsh and I put the tape recorder in the car without him appearing to notice. We discussed matters in general, and he chuckled; clearly something amused him so I asked him why. It transpired that I had parked my car near the home of a lady who was in the habit of entertaining a number of boy-friends and my friend the policeman concluded that I was one of them. I did not know the lady, or even of her existence, but it was convenient not to disabuse him of this misconception and we parted with mutual good wishes. The tape recording was most revealing and was used to good effect, sufficiently at least to ensure that the speaker was removed from the lecture circuit.

About this time a certain reverend gentleman, who was also a member of the Blaenau UDC, saw fit to attack the Railway from the pulpit, which stupid, not to say irreverent action was indicative of the feeling being fostered in Blaenau by the BEA propoganda.

The Railway, having had no traffic for eight years, was heavily overgrown from Tan-y-Bwlch to Boston Lodge; it was most heartening to see the many volunteers who came under the Society's auspices from all over the country to work on the clearance at weekends. One day, while working on the line just below Penrhyn, a lady from a house beside the line invited me in to have a cup of tea and to meet her invalid husband who told me that he was the guard on the official train taking the Inspecting Officer of Railways through the Aberglaslyn Pass prior to opening the Welsh Highland Railway; he said that the train was propelled slowly through the tunnels with the doors wide open to check on clearances.

The volunteers formed a cross-section of all types of skills and professions; early on I had a visit from one Norman Pearce who had been to see Garraway who had been too preoccupied to talk. Norman was offering to re-instate the telephone lines and to provide instruments and materials; we were obviously not in a position to accept such help at the time but I saw to it that he was put in touch with Les Smith and he became, as is well known, a most important figure in the Society and the Company.

We also had Dr Brian Rogers (father of Seamus), Robin Butterell and Peter Hollins, the latter two being architects. We reinstated the very dilapidated roof of the Booking Office and open shelter at Minffordd Station, which was open to the sky! The original was in decorative slate and as funds did not allow reinstatement in slate, fancy or otherwise, we re-roofed it in corrugated asbestos and painted it grey to make it less obtrusive.

A variety of people and firms were very helpful to the Railway. Cooke's Explosives at that time had a small works at Cwm Nantcol where they manufactured sodium chlorate, as well as the works at Penrhyn. They were very generous in supplying this weed-killer. Hempel's Paint also donated supplies of their product and sold us more of it very reasonably.

As Engineer for Ways and Works I conscripted friends who were experienced Civil Engineers to walk the line with me to inspect the walls and embankments; I had an unreasonable phobia about Cei Mawr, having witnessed the effect of trapped water and frost on a structure in the north of England. I abseiled down each face to place glass "tell tales" which, to my immense relief remained intact. This was my first and last "abseil" as I have no head for height and was secretly terrified, and also deeply ashamed; I felt as though I had questioned the professional integrity of James Spooner.

The state of over-bridges, under-bridges and foot-bridges, especially between Tanygrisiau and Duffws, which had been neglected for so many years, was admittedly deplorable. Suddenly the Urban District Council became aware of the terrible dangers to the public and began to demand their urgent and immediate repair. I believe the potential danger to the public increased ten-fold overnight as soon as the unscrupulous financiers and the naughty little train-playing boys acquired control of the Company. The suggestion was even made that the Council were consulting the BEA whenever they wrote to us! As money was very short, I made what efforts I could to satisfy the local authority with minimum expenditure by the Company.

With the severance of the track below Tanygrisiau, the whole future of the line above it was in balance and, naturally, Bill Bellamy was most cautious regarding expenditure. The entire position was made more difficult by the shortage of contractors available to do the work, but we were lucky to have one or two one-man firms who did odd jobs at very reasonable rates; in retrospect I am more than ever convinced that the Council's concern was more with harassing the Company rather than with any real concern for public safety.

I received one letter from a private individual, in Welsh, saying that he understood that the Railway had now been taken over by "pobl ac arian", "people with money". He asked if they would be prepared to pay for a bullock he had lost which had fallen though a footbridge that the company had failed to maintain. It appears that it was his driving the animal across the pedestrian bridge that was the cause of its collapse; needless to say he did not even get a reply.

It was a pretty hopeless task trying to persuade the Blaenau public that they could have the Power Station AND the Railway; the propaganda of the BEA had been too intense. The BEA's representatives met members of the Company to discuss possible diversions round the reservoir; we met them, with the Simplex and the brake van at Tanygrisiau and ran through for a site meeting at the south end of the tunnel (having frantically removed an obstruction which had fallen from one of the air shafts the previous weekend). This meeting was shortly followed by a meeting between the BEA and the County Council at which the FR was not represented; here, the BEA insisted that a tunnel would be required from near Dduallt to a point on the Blaenau side of the new power station. This was clearly ludicrous both in engineering and cost terms but it was obviously put across to justify the BEA's line of "no diversion for the Railway".

The long-sustained brain-washing by the BEA I think engendered in their officials, and certainly in my own forebodings, the idea that the hydro proposals would be approved as a matter of routine by the Merioneth County Council; however our own propaganda, if such it could be called, was beginning to have some effect. The Welsh Press was favourable and such headlines as "Lein Bach will open up new tourist era" showed that other carrots existed as well as the hydro-electric type. This one attribute to Tom Lloyd Jones and his boss Geoff Charles of *Y Cymro* ; also to the late Hughie Roberts of Barmouth, who was a most delightful character as well as a regional reporter both for the provincial daily *The Liverpool Daily Post* and for the dear old *Cambrian News*, which did its share in publicising the revival. In addition some favourable pieces appeared in the national dailies such as the *Daily Telegraph*.

We also had supporters among the County Council, notable among them being Alderman R.O.Wynne of Ffestiniog; he had the perspicacity to see that the hydro-scheme and the Railway were not mutually exclusive, except in BEA propaganda, and he did not hesitate to say so in unambiguous terms. He had a particular dislike of the way in which the electricity authorities spewed out power lines and he referred sarcastically to his neighbouring beautiful landscape of Cwm Cynfal, where they had proliferated, as "Poland"! One evening I arranged for Trevor Bailey, Les Smith and Bill Broadbent to visit him and they ably stated the Ffestiniog's case, reinforcing his determination to do all he could to secure the benefits of both projects.

A week or so before the County Council's meeting, its Clerk, Dafydd Jones Williams, rang me to ask if I would arrange an informal meeting between him and the representatives of the Company; he was an official of great acumen and balance who later became the Welsh "Ombudsman". It was clear that in order to advise his Council he wanted to weigh up the sincerity and calibre of the Ffestiniog side, so I arranged a meeting at my home in Dolgellau where he met the same representatives (Bailey, Smith and Broadbent) and they gave an excellent account of themselves which I am certain was an important factor in the Council's decision to oppose the proposal. Although this was only in the nature of a holding operation it gave more time to weigh up the situation and for the Ffestiniog to further marshal its forces.

I began to patrol the line, particularly from the tunnel up, and to try to trace items stolen and to check vandalism in general. Not much was recovered but it served some purpose as people became aware that someone was looking after the interests of the Company. I had first-class cooperation from the Police, in particular Inspector Lewis Jones who was in charge at Blaenau and also Sergeant Evans and a great character PC Davies of Tanygrisiau who accompanied me on many a reconnaissance through the tunnel and we hit on an ingenious way to avoid getting our feet wet by walking in parallel on the rail tops and intertwining our arms to keep our balance.

A great deal had been stolen from the Railway during the period of closure, and even afterwards. We had much trouble with one scrap merchant who, it was thought, removed a number of items including even Fairlie loco parts, that he was not supposed to. I was very worried once when a lorry loaded with chairs was seen going through Dolgellau, but they turned out to be standard-gauge ones!

I also came to know the Reverend Richard Griffiths who was the Congregational Minister at Tanygrisiau; he told me how he had officiated at a funeral of an occupant of Tunnel Cotage when the line was closed, the coffin being put on a trolley and being pushed to Tanygrisiau to be loaded onto a hearse.

In March 1955 I was instructed to conduct one Mr Layzell, an assessor who was acting for the Company's insurers, over the line. I was frankly apprehensive as to what he might think! It must be remembered that the line was in keyed rail throughout, with most of the keys missing. In the event, on 24th March 1955, I had Arwyn Morgan and a companion, both being apprentices at Boston Lodge, standing by at the Lodge with the Simplex and a brake van (the famous No. 7) and we set off upline at about 10.15am. We stopped at several points for Mr Layzell to make inspections and arrived at Glan-y-Pwll at about 1pm. We had lunch at the "North Western Hotel" and we then inspected the Glan-y-Pwll to Duffws section on foot, rejoining the "special train" at Glan-y-Pwll about 3pm. We set off back to Boston Lodge and, to my great relief, Arwyn brought us back without incident. It was with intense relief that I dined with Mr Layzell that night at the "Sportsman"; I have not seen Arwyn since those days except on television when he was conducting a choir!

29. *Simplex and no. 11 wait to leave on a line clearance trip to Tunnel South in June 1955. The scene was repeated many times that year. (RC)*

30. *The platform withstood the unexpected arrival of lorries. The ex-BR sleepers are being loaded onto the frame of a former Hudson open coach in February 1955. (RWFS)*

31. Also recorded in February 1955 was coach no. 10, which became a veteran of many body-battering trips through the undergrowth. (RWFS)

32. Simplex returns from Boston Lodge on 27th July 1955, the Wednesday of the first week of operation. The grass had grown well since the winter clearance. (JD)

33. More tidying took place before the general manager's MG TC was photographed on 26th October 1955. An oil lamp was still in place. (ALlL)

34. Harbour bush clearance was still in progress in November 1954, while hard-working FRS secretary F.Gilbert (left) looked on. (RWFS)

❧ Mike Elvy ❧

At the end of August 1954, six of us from the school set up camp near Boston Lodge Works with the intention of doing some line clearance work. Most of the work we did in those early days was cutting trees and vegetation and stacking it in places where it could later be tipped clear of the track. We had a few axes and spades for cutting away the wild growth from the track. Our most useful bit of equipment though, was an old waggon frame on wheels we had found. This we used for carting rubbish to the stacking locations - because of wet weather it was virtually impossible to burn rubbish. We also used our old waggon frame as a battering ram to cut down the undergrowth. Later we acquired a box van to fit on our wheeled frame. It was great for carrying things - and as a dry place where we could sit and eat our sandwiches.

One day Robert Evans, the old General Manager of the Festiniog who had been retained to look after the railway's assets, came over to show us round the Boston Lodge Works. He pointed out the terrible condition of just everything and told us we were wasting our time and that the railway would never run again.

At the end of our time we had not made a great impression on clearing the whole length to the old Minffordd station, but at least we had done well along the section to Minffordd cemetery.

Following the success of our initial effort, Allan Garraway, an engineer from British Railways Eastern Region became involved in organising the restoration. Enthusiasts started to go up there for weekends of voluntary work. Most travelled by car, but I learned from Allan that it was possible to travel by train from London after work on Fridays, get in a good twenty-four hours restoration work, and be back in London early on a Monday morning. I was then working for British Railways and was entitled to 'privilege tickets' - tickets issued to railway staff at one quarter normal fare. So, some weekends I travelled out to Portmadoc by train. But it was not the easiest of journeys and involved a middle of the night change at Crewe. All the same, we did it, and got through a lot of work clearing up the line around Boston Lodge and tidying up the workshop area; and then the old workshop foreman, Morris Jones, got interested and came to help. Invaluable help; help that very quickly had the Simplex petrol locomotive working.

I left BR in September 1955 to go to college, but before starting I had a few weeks to spare, so back I went to Portmadoc to do some work and to see how the railway project was progressing. And, wonder of wonders, trains were already running along the railway that Robert Evans had said 'would never run again'.

During those few weeks before returning to college I did a variety of work, occasionally helping with the running of the train. One day I went up on the Simplex with Allan and a few others to Blaenau Ffestinog to collect some of the old slate waggons which had been abandoned up there and bring them down for scrap. It was an interesting, and hairy, trip. Especially so going through Moelwyn tunnel - a tunnel which seemed to fit the train like a glove. On arriving back at Minffordd, we discovered that some of the slate waggons had LNWR inscribed axle boxes - quite a find for railway enthusiasts. And so I went back to college, exhausted and happy in the knowledge that after all the hard work, a dream was at last beginning to come true.

35. *Moments later and the Simplex was recorded with AGWG driving and LAHH standing beside him. Mr. Nelson is on the left. (RWFS)*

36. *Although Barbara (Mitchell to be) launched the FRS publicly at Easter 1955, it was to be 30th July before she saw a train. The Simplex had been turned by that time. (VM)*

37. **Prince** *was recorded from the top of a bus on its third day in use, 6th August 1955. (VM)*

38. *September 1955 and* **Prince** *had brought a load of scrap across the Cob behind the empty coaches. It is about to shunt them onto the WHR connection for the material to be unloaded, probably by the foundry staff. (RWFS)*

❧ Norman Gurley ❧

I joined the Society during the winter of 1954/55 and received Newsletter No. 2 in which there was an appeal for an envelope addresser. The Secretary, a Leonard Heath Humphrys, arranged to meet me at Watford (Met) Station to discuss my application. I never heard whether there were any others. For some reason I was expecting a tall, angular, middle-aged gent in sports jacket with leather elbows. The leather elbows seemed most important! So I took no notice of the very young man in a smart business suit. Fortunately Len had no preconceived notions about me and we were soon relaxing in the family sitting room, deciding that my title should be Hon. Distribution Manager. I was to hold this title for nearly 42 years. My first envelopes were addressed in long-hand with turquoise-blue ink in my fountain pen. I wonder if any readers remember it. Newsletters were issued at irregular intervals when someone found time to write one and I did not have much to do that summer.

We asked my father about the possibility of using his (Whitbread fleet) car for working parties and, to my surprise, found that he was agreeable and that Whitbread rules would permit it at weekends. Organising a trip was another matter for Len was a busy young man and I knew no one else who would be interested. Eventually my first working party took off from Watford Junction Station on the evening of Friday July 29th 1955. My four passengers were Len Heath Humphrys and Vic Mitchell, both of the 1951 "Bristol Meeting", Barbara Fisk (Mitchell from 1958 onwards) and vivacious, black-haired Barbara Spice, secretary to Geoff Sumpster, who had taken on the job of Secretary to the newly-formed Festiniog Railway Society Limited. By Shrewsbury we had had enough of the A5 and we travelled via Welshpool and Dolgelly, arriving in Portmadoc around 07.15.

It was a still, sunny morning and Portmadoc Harbour offered reflections I have rarely seen since. Perhaps it was too early in the morning for the sewage outfalls to ruffle the water. After I had been introduced to Mrs Owen and Vera McMillan, and enjoyed my first breakfast at the Commercial Hotel, we reported to Harbour Station. I was put to work with some other individuals changing joint sleepers on the Cob, while the Simplex rattled past with two coach loads of happy holiday-makers at regular intervals. The train service had started on July 23rd and the line had been officially declared open by the Wales Tourist Board Queen, Janet Jones, before we had set off on the Friday. Later on the Saturday Vic journeyed to join his parents who were on holiday at Barmouth.

After dinner Len and I joined a trip up the line with Allan Garraway at the controls of the Simplex. The loco's magneto had long since decided it was time for bed and it was a stop-start journey. It stalled near Dduallt Manor and we had to push down-hill so that Allan had room to wield the monster starting handle. Was it by accident or design that it had to be inserted on the valley side? Eventually we entered Moelwyn Tunnel but it was late and dark and a new rock-fall halted further progress. That was the furthest that I travelled up the old line. It was customary to take Mr Owen of the Commercial Hotel on such outings so that nobody got locked out!

In those days August Bank Holiday was on the first Monday in August and in 1955 August 1st was the Monday, so I had Sunday changing sleepers and then spent the evening helping to demolish the war-time block-post which was restricting the loading gauge at the Boston Lodge end of the Cob. On Monday I drove home via Towyn with Len and Barbara, with the sun still shining. I learned later that *Prince* ran trials on the Tuesday and began passenger service on the Wednesday.

Memories are hazy but I think I drove to Portmadoc about four weeks later with the Company's Publicity Man, Blanco White and his USA friend Lee Dietricht. We explored the Glyn Valley Tramway on the outward journey and had a lengthy stop at Llanberis on our way home, but I remember nothing at all about what happened in between. I must have visited the FR as I have a couple of unexciting slides of *Prince* on the Cob with two carriages.

I travelled to Portmadoc by minibus with members of the embryo London Area Group in order to attend the first meeting of the Society on October 8th in the wonderful, old Town Hall building. This was condemned and demolished soon afterwards and was eventually replaced by Woolworths. The Commercial was full and we stayed in a couple of cramped rooms at the Ship Inn, Lombard Street. The noises from the bar kept me awake for all of five minutes! Three people mentioned in the meeting: L.A.H.H., David Cole and Lillian Coombs, all became LAG committee members and I was the first secretary of the Group. On the Sunday we walked from Tanygrisiau to the Moelwyn Tunnel and back before heading home.

39. The station presented a reasonably tidy sight by August 1955, but the permanent way did not warrant close examination. (AGWG)

40. **Prince** departs in August 1955, while a man stands on the long-disused WHR connection in the background. (JBS)

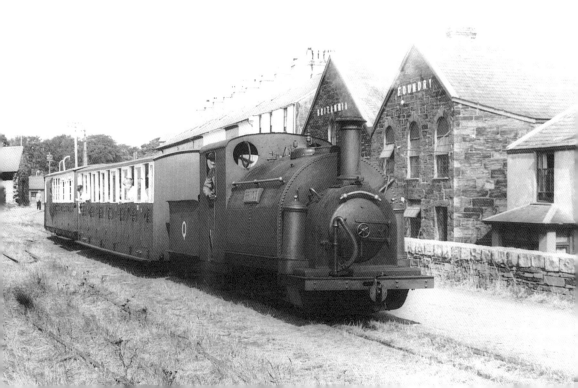

ಎ Len Heath Humphrys ಎ

By 1951, many better people than I had tried, and were still trying to do something about the tragic, pathetic silence that reigned supreme along the line.

Perhaps they were all too hampered by their accountants to succeed, for even if one had only a very elementary knowledge of accounts, the Railway Company's liabilities, were enough to make even the stoutest heart wilt - some £39,000 odd in debentures, loans and bank overdraft for a start, not to mention many other debts! It is not surprising that all those who approached the railway with "honourable intentions" took one look at these frightening facts and decided that although they would like to buy the railway, they did not want the Company's tremendous labililties.

Of the many who were interested at one time or another were such well known people as Mr J.I.C.Boyd and Mr P.B.Whitehouse, Mr R.C.S.Lowe and Mr W.B.Broadbent, the Society's Chairman. To all these people, the same stumbling block presented itself - the Railway Company's financial tangle. The then Directors were not easy people to deal with; they had originally purchased their shares as a speculation just before the 1914/18 war, and I suppose they must have spent many wasted hours with interested callers who shuddered at the financial problems, and disappeared! Perhaps the old FR Board was not completely to blame for the apathy which enveloped the railway at this time.

When the revival of the line was first mooted, no one gave consideration to a situation such as was to be found in 1946/50. If they had, I might have had a different story to write today - perhaps another Lynton & Barnstaple tragedy?

Perhaps you will understand all these remarks when I say that the Festiniog Railway Company has no power to abandon its undertaking, sell its line - or even lease it, except to the Welsh Highland (Light Railway) Company. It was therefore not possible for someone to purchase the railway and leave the "Old Railway Company" to rot away in the background. It was for the same reasons that the Minister of Transport was prevented from granting the Company a Warrant of Abandonment in November, 1950; hence our existence today.

My interest in the Festiniog was first aroused in 1949 by David Balantine, a friend with whom I subsequently lost touch. It was he who infected me with the fascination of the narrow gauge, via Lee's Narrow Gauge Railways in North Wales. The idea of a rehabilitation fund occurred to me early in 1950, an idea which I suggested to a well known railway magazine in March of that year. It was not greeted with enthusiasm - needless to say, I now know why!

It was in July, 1950 that I had my first contact with the Festiniog Railway Company and at this stage I had not heard of any suggestion to form a Preservation Society for the Talyllyn Railway. The idea of a Society to re-open the Festiniog was, as far as I am concerned, original, and at the time I thought that as there were many thousands of railway enthusiasts in the country, there must be quite a few who would join such a venture. My enthusiasm was not always shared; one club president pointed out that the SLS had had difficulty in raising cash to preserve *Gladstone*, what hope had I of raising enough money for a railway. Such a state of affairs in these days of a multiplicity of Preservation Societies, all of which seem to attract a sufficient number of adherents, appears downright ludicrous.

In October 1950 with these thoughts uppermost in my mind, I re-visited the "Land of our Fathers", which had been my home during the war when my "father" was works superintendent at the Saunders Roe Shadow Factory in Anglesey. After visiting the famous quarries of Penrhyn and Padarn I eventually arrived at Portmadoc - it was "raining"! My visit was short, but I saw sufficient to realise that "here was something worth fighting for".

Readers may be surprised to learn that I was only 17 years old at the time. Perhaps if I had been older and had really realised the seriousness of the Company's financial position and of the whole proposal, I would never have dared to put pen to paper! However, ignorance was bliss in this case, and fools rush in where angels fear to tread. Although my actions may have appeared slightly rash, it must, of course, be remembered that the railway was not completely dead. A considerable goods traffic was handled by the Festiniog, and during this period (1950/51), with property, rents, etc., yielded a four figure annual income.

The following day I visited the Talyllyn Railway, fearing that I was to see it on its last day of operation, and I now value a complete collection of the last tickets actually issued on that day. I am pleased to say that my fears were not justified, and it was on the Talyllyn train that I first made the acquaintance of Mr G.H.Walker. He informed me of the Talyllyn Railway Preservation proposals. The day after this, I walked the length of the Talyllyn, and the memory of that walk, along an almost non-existent track, kept to gauge by turf and bits of slate, and, in many parts lacking sleepers, contributed more than anything else to keeping up my spirit through the many weary years that were to precede the revival of the Festiniog.

In November/December 1950 I wrote to those whom I knew to be interested in the Festiniog Railway's revival, and again to the Railway Company. Strange to say, the replies I received were completely opposed to each other. One side said, "there is no hope of re-opening the railway; the Railway Company will not co-operate"; however, this pessimistic view was not shared by the Railway Company itself, which offered every co-operation! In response to further correspondence with the Company's secretary in January, 1951 I was able to form an opinion of the way in which the line would have to be taken over and of its outstanding liabilities.

The first published reference to my efforts appeared in the January 1951 *Journal of the British Locomotive Society* - it produced two replies! However, it was noticed, for a short, although inaccurate, editorial comment appeared in the correspondence columns of the March *Trains Illustrated*. This produced twenty-two interested correspondents.

I realised right from the start that, at least initially, I required the help of professional engineers and railwaymen rather than of ordinary enthusiasts. With this in mind I approached the editors of the *Railway Gazette*, The *Engineer and Engineering*, all of whom were kind enough to publish my letter asking for assistance. This put me in touch with a further forty-eight enthusiasts, of whom many were later to contribute substantially to the success of the effort to revive the Festiniog Railway.

In April 1951 I again visited the line and Boston Lodge and was heartened by what I saw as compared with the Pendre "works" and the rest of the Talyllyn Railway when I had been there the previous October. However, it was at this time that the first of the checks in progress came. The Portmadoc Urban District Council called a meeting of interested parties on 20th April 1951, (in Vol. 2 of the History of the Festiniog Railway, page 345, this date is given as 1950), which, as Mr J.I.C.Boyd relates, was not a success, although a committee was, in fact, formed. It was very clear, however, that those present from Portmadoc had expected the railway enthusiasts at the meeting to come out with a cut and dried plan complete with the "cut and dried" cash to go with it.

Waiting for the committee to act involved a frustrating delay, but as soon as it became apparent that nothing was to come out of the Portmadoc meeting, I called the now famous "Bristol meeting". This was held in the Club Rooms of the Bristol Railway Circle and formed what was, for some odd reason, known as the "Bath Committee". This meeting was memorable for me, and perhaps one of the things I remember most was the fact that I was late arriving, to be greeted by a group of twelve people seated in anticipation around an empty table. Although twelve may sound a small number, I think I can say that each was a true-blooded narrow gauge enthusiast, all of whom had travelled many miles to be in Bristol. Of the twelve, the names of Allan Garraway, John Bate, F.Gilbert, R.W.Winter, H.Holcroft and Victor Mitchell will, I am sure, be known to most of you for their activities at some time or another in the narrow gauge field.

The Bristol meeting resulted in a second meeting being arranged in the London area, at the "Old Bull" Inn, Barnet, a month later on 8th October. This meeting really put things on a firm basis and, realising that legalities were going to be amongst its chief troubles, formed a Legal Committee. This committee came under the wing of Mr F.Gilbert who, with the untiring help of his solicitor, Mr L.Taylor Harris, was to become the backbone of the Festiniog Railway Society.

The story continues but I will rest here, for what took place at the meetings and thereafter was a combined effort and must be the subject of a separate article. In conclusion I should like to take this opportunity of thanking all who wrote in those early days - every letter was an encouragement. Thank you.

41. *The historic moment of the first movement since 1946 was recorded on 21st September 1954 as the Simplex reached the gates of Boston Lodge Works. (RWFS)*

42. *The gate pillars are in the background in this view of Boston Lodge Works and its Long Shed from 20th February 1955. (AGWG)*

43. *Managers old and new are central in this memorable view from 22nd September 1954. (RWFS)*

44. *Moving on to 21st October 1954, we witness another train of scrap. It included Morris Jones' old car, which had featured in many interior photograhs of the Works during the closure period. (RWFS)*

*45. Volunteers gather round **Busta** on 23rd January 1955, with its guardian, Ian Smart, second from the right. (AGWG)*

46. The yard was subject to difficult conditions on 20th February 1955. Such weather was uncommon at this end of the line. (AGWG)

✎ Peter Jamieson ✎

My conversion had come in 1952 when, like many another, I had come across the forlorn remains of wagons and the elegant bogie brake in the grass-grown sidings at Harbour Station.

There followed visits with a friend who shared my passion. Together we braved the Welsh weather on bicycles, often clad in oily capes and sou'westers. We walked the line, shoes waterlogged, and took photographs with old box cameras, and somehow found our way into Boston Lodge, where on one occasion we had an audience with Allan Garraway, who was inspecting his future demesne.

When, early in 1955, the Society started to enrol the faithful, I joined up, No 55 (I think), and made plans to cycle, yet again, to Wales. In those days before motorway madness, the main roads were mostly two lane and lined with telegraph poles. The youth hostels were spartan and it required stamina and determination to cross the Welsh hills on a bike.

And so, after a night at Harlech Hostel, I had arrived and was standing on the platform at Harbour Station. Far out across the Cob I could see a wisp of steam and a plume of sulphurous smoke approaching at a snail's pace. Eventually *Prince* and two coaches passed the old gantry signal and gingerly took the super-elevated curve into the platform. It was a great moment.

I had written from school, offering my services to the Company, and Allan Garraway had replied saying he would put me on 'deturfing', a task which at that time could absorb volunteers without number. In fact, I found myself deputed to help Fred Boughey shore up the old engine pit in the works yard, which, being lined with rotten wood, had partially collapsed under *Prince* who had been parked there quietly one lunch time. It was hot work, but not taxing and we refreshed ourselves with bottles of dandelion & burdock, brought across the Cob on the train.

Lunch was taken on the beach at Pen Cob and might be followed by a swim. The height of luxury was, however, to have lunch at the Commercial Hotel, where you could feel replete for 1/6d.

But all too soon it was time to start for home, and so, spiritually refreshed, I set my Sturmy Archer three speed gear at the road to Bala and the border, resting on the way at Blodwell Junction, Kinnerley and Snailbeach - all now of blessed memory.

Trains using the old tunnel in 1955 - Compiled by Allan Garraway

31 January	*Simplex*	*Glan-y-Pwll*	*Survey*
5 February	*Simplex*	*LMR Station*	*CEA meeting*
5 March	*Simplex*	*Dyffws*	*Track clearance*
23 July	*Simplex*	*Tanygrisiau*	*Reopening celebration*
1 August	*Busta*	*Blaenau*	*Press officer*
31 August	*Simplex*	*Blaenau*	*Collect wagons*
27 September	*Simplex*	*Blaenau*	*Collect wagons*
31 October	*Simplex*	*Blaenau*	*Collect wagons*

*47a. The gudgeon pins for **Prince** were machined on this ancient belt-driven lathe. (JLA)*

47b. The Crossley engine was the only source of power for restoration work initially. (JLA)

48. This volume would be incomplete without record of some of the historic treasures saved, such as the Cleminson wagon with sliding centre axle and radial outer ones. (RWFS)

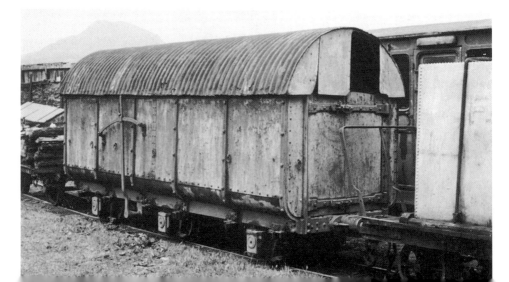

49. The horse dandy used in pre-steam days was another historic item saved for posterity and is seen with an early type of slate wagon. (RWFS)

50. Beyond saving and seen in Top Yard in May 1955 was this van, which had been more often photographed in Harbour Station. "Turtle Roof" was the term widely used by Victorian coach builders, but not in FR records. (RWFS)

✺ Vic Mitchell ✺

I became a keen railway observer from an early age, having been born and bred within sight of the Southern Railway at Hampton. A narrow gauge addiction started with the lovely Kerr Stuarts on the Metropolitan Water Board's railway from there to Kempton Park.

Cigarette cards were not produced during the war, but they became collectors items amongst school lads and life stopped when I came across one depicting a double Fairlie. I resolved to see the real thing running and was devastated to read in 1946 that there would be no hope of fulfilling this ambition.

Having read more about this unique railway, I set off to examine it the day after I left school in July 1951. I went with Alan French, the only boy in the school with his own steam engine, albeit only O gauge. We stayed overnight in the Youth Hostel at Pont-y-Pant, close to the station on the Conway Valley branch.

To compound our amazement at emerging from the astonishingly long tunnel next morning into a town surrounded by grey walls topped by a ceiling of grey cloud, we found that the FR was not closed. Our euphoria was short lived however, when we realised that we were walking in the wrong direction, towards a quarry.

Turning round, we set off along the main line, over Glan-y-Pwll crossing, and soon found a wagon apparently abandoned on the track. We requisitioned this for the conveyance of our rucksacks and embarked on the greatest adventure of our lives (to date). In over-ambitious youthful mode, we could see no reason why we should not reopen the line, as we gleefully propelled our wagon. Our joy was soon interrupted by a shout coming from a raised fist to the effect "that wagon is not yours". We agreed to return it later, but we could not find it when we went back (in 1956) to keep our promise.

At Tan-y-Bwlch everything was surprisingly neat and tidy, the top points had clearly been oiled recently. The way onwards seemed impenetrable and so we resolved to continue by bus. Just missing it, we used our thumbs. A lorry stopped: "jump up the back", said the driver with a grin, knowing how painful it would be to sit on a load of slates edge on! His destination was Minffordd Yard, precisely ours.

The survey here complete, we walked to Boston Lodge and made further mental notes but could not gain access. Our visit ended amongst the relics at Harbour station. By evening we were pitching our small tent at Towyn, where we became some of the first PW volunteers. Mr Rolt told us quite firmly to forget the FR, as there was room for only one preserved railway in Britain.

I had been in correspondence with Leonard Heath Humphrys since April; we both used "Dear Sir" and "Yours faithfully". It was not until the Bristol meeting in September that I realised that he was also only 17! I was actively involved in the campaign with him in London thereafter and became a FRS director on 1st October 1955; five others were co-opted at the same time.

The details of the acquisition have been recounted elsewhere and were not my immediate concern. However, I was involved with the public presentation scheme at Eastertide in 1955. We took a stand at the Model Railway Club Exhibition in Central Hall, Westminster, with the intention of showing some FR models. I suggested that the only type of models that interested press photographers were those in skirts. The retort was "where could we get one?" Well, I am engaged to one", I said. "Dress her up as a Welsh station mistress" chirped up an alert member.

A suitable costume was obtained by Leonard H-H, but Barbara had the problem of deciding where to apply the various parts. The plan was successful and she appeared on the front page of both daily papers in Wales. It was just as well that her boss did not read them, as he thought she had a dental appointment that morning. It was a partial truth, as I was a dental student. The six-year course, mostly 50 weeks per year, left no time for work on the FR, but most of the admin was in London and so I was actively involved in this instead.

51. Boston Lodge Halt is the scene for this serious conversation between Lt. Col. McMullen and Mr. L.J.W.Smith during the critical MOT inspection on 21st July 1955. (MS)

52. After terminating at Boston Lodge Halt, the train had to reverse to the points near the Yard gates where a chain was used to shunt the coaches past the locomotive. (JBS)

53. **Prince** *is seen from the top of a gate pillar in September 1955. The building was once a signal box and housed the point levers. (RWFS)*

54. *The original loco shed was not used for operational purposes after the takeover. No. 11 is outside it in about April 1955. (RWFS)*

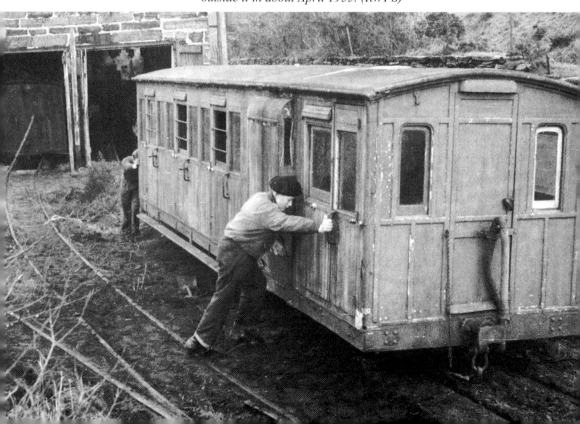

✧ Arwyn Morgan ✧

It was November 1954 when I became an employee of the railway, having previously been with Saunders Roe, Anglesey. There was no mains electricity or water at Boston Lodge, and water for tea was obtained from a stream by the loco shed. Heating was by brazier and lighting by duck lamps. My first job was to remove the brass mountings off *Palmerston*, which stood outside the blacksmith shop and was used to power the steam hammer.

The clack box and mountings were then stored in the small office in the erecting shop; but just before Christmas, this was broken into and the mountings were stolen. I had to go through the same process again, removing mountings from *Princess* and *Welsh Pony*, situated in the loco shed.

The mountings were then assembled on the new boiler of *Prince*; holes were scribed and centres punched. I borrowed an oxy/acetylene cutter from the Glaslyn Foundry to burn holes for outlets for steam and water inlets. As there was no electricity, I mounted a swan neck and ratchet drill to bore the holes - very tedious as holes were to be drilled to the profile of the fire box. There were approximately 18 holes and these were then tapped to receive ½ inch dia. studs. The clack box studs were also drilled and tapped using the same method.

Jointing for these mountings consisted of white lead, red lead, brass gauze and lead wire woven around the steam/water outlet/inlet. Morris insisted on this old fashioned method, although I preferred "Walkerite", having used it on joints at my previous employment at Saunders Roe but Morris still insisted on his method.

The source of power for the machine shop was a Crossley hot bulb single cylinder engine. However, the paraffin blow lamp did not generate sufficient heat for a hot plug start so I unscrewed the plug, heated in the open forge and then ran with it in tongs and replaced it, tightening it with a spanner. With Morris on the fuel hand pump and myself turning the engine we would bring it to life.

After a time, the thread on the plug burnt away and one day there was an almighty bang. The plug flew out and struck Fred Boughey just as he was entering the erecting shop from the old joiners shop. Fortunately, he was struck on his body and not his head. At times the Crossley would race away - one had to hang on to the fuel pump handle to stop the engine. By this time the whole erecting shop was vibrating!

We were all working hard to get *Prince* ready for the official opening on 23rd July 1955. I had worked all day on 22nd July and was asked to work the night to get *Prince* in steam.

To save time we decided to burn holes in the footplate to secure the cab. The FR had purchased oxy/acetylene by this time and I was burning the holes. Work got on well until we came to the drivers side when I asked Allan Garraway, "Where's the next?" Allan pointed out the position and at that exact moment I moved my torch over Allan's hand. There was an almight howl. I had burnt the back of his hand and at that moment my name was changed!

By next morning *Prince* had been moved out to the yard, lit and was gaining steam pressure. It started to "blow off" and I attempted to turn on the one and only injector. It failed after numerous attempts and as the water was very low in the glass, I dropped the fire. We investigated the failure after letting the water out from the tank.

I removed the injector and found that the water hole in the Walkerite jointing had not been cut out. This was due to my failure to pay attention to detail. Thus, the Simplex was prepared for the official opening.

It was a real good old "work-horse", often off the road and often stalled, but nevertheless Allan Garraway kept it going. The Rev Timothy Philips, who in the 46/54 era was a volunteer caretaker to Boston Lodge composed an "englyn" to the "Simplex" (a metrical alliteration and unique):

Di-nam yw'r peiriant gwamal, - a Morus
ymyrodd yn ddyfal;
Eto os na bydd atal -
Garraway a'i gyrr i'r wal

Over meek little weaklin' - a worried
Morris kept thinkin'
Garraway can try brakin'
He'll smash walls and loose machine".

55. Other coaches to survive under cover in reasonable condition were two of the original four-wheelers from about 1865. (RWFS)

56. Return empties! Simplex is taking gas bottles back to the Harbour on 26th October 1955 and is passing the shell of the signal box. (ALlL)

Should the FR abandon a myth?

It is an established part of FR tradition that one of the reasons why the railway exists today is because the Festiniog Act of 1832 (and subsequent Acts) contained no power of abandonment.

The facts are well known. In November 1950 the Company was in dire financial circumstances and the country's scrap merchants were gathering. On 9th November 1950 the company resolved in a general meeting to apply to the Ministry of Transport for an Abandonment Order that was then refused. Boyd sums up the position: 'the deadlock was obvious' - it required an Act of Parliament to abandon the Festiniog Railway - and that was the only way out of it.

John Winton is more graphic: 'The company was caught in an impasse... The railway could not be leased. Those who owned it did not want it but could not get rid of it'.

The purpose of an Abandonment Order is that it releases the Railway Company from the statutory obligations to construct, maintain or operate the railway. No buyer would purchase the company unless those obligations (and the related compensation penalties) were released by the Warrant of Abandonment.

The Company had actually made matters worse by applying for an Order. Once an application was made the powers of the directors to pay debts or enter into contract with respect to the railway were restricted.

This note submits that James Boyd and John Winton are wrong. It is suggested that there were three courses of action open to the company, (and its creditors) in 1950, which if properly investigated and pursued could have led to the loss of the FR.

Firstly, it was possible to apply for a further Act of Parliament but at a cost beyond the means of the company. The Swansea and Mumbles Railway Company Ltd was dissolved by the South Wales Transport Act 1959.

Secondly, the Ministry of Transport could have granted an Abandonment Order under the Abandonment of Railways Act 1850. If it were right (as suggested by Boyd) that the Ministry advised that no Order could be made because the railway had been opened for public traffic, then that is a misunderstanding of the Act. Section 8 of the Act allowed a creditor, who had obtained a judgement, to apply for an Abandonment Order, provided that no part of the railway had been opened for traffic. No such restriction applied to the Festiniog Railway Company, who satisfied the criteria for the grant of a warrant of abandonment.

Thirdly, the company or any creditor could have applied to the Court for an order winding up the Company. A statutory company (the FR) could not be wound up like an ordinary stock company (unless it had obtained a Warrant of Abandonment). However, under the 1948 Companies Act the FR could have been voluntarily registered under the 1948 Act. Once registered the company could then have been wound up by an application to the Court. Both the registration and the application for a winding up order are relatively straightforward procedures.

It is therefore suggested that the FR was in a more perilous position in 1950 than our tradition suggests. If a further Act of Parliament was beyond the means of the Company there were two further courses of action that could have been followed. We should be very grateful that creditors and company alike did not look too carefully at the real options open to them in those financially strained days of 1950. Had they done so then those who led the present administration might have had a more difficult and maybe an impossible task.

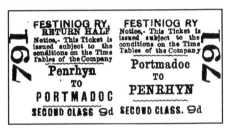

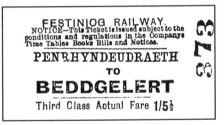

57. Nearest is one of the first bogie coaches in the world; it is no. 15. The van has been seen in picture no. 50. (RWFS)

58. The great length of the engine shed is evident in this October 1954 view. Also included are the water tank and the smoke vents. (RWFS)

❧ Alan Pegler ❧

It all started, so far as I was concerned, with two steam specials on the Eastern Region in 1950 and 1952. On the first of these I met the late Earl of Northesk, who told me of the Festiniog Railway's plight; on the second I was with my old friend Trevor Bailey and a wartime friend of his, Leslie Smith. We had all joined forces to run what became a quite famous "special", the Centenaries Express.

Les worked for the Finchley Council whose Surveyor at that time was Tommy King, one of the original Festiniog Society Committee who, in his turn, had been co-opted by his friend F.Gilbert, a builder with strong sentimental attachments to North Wales.

Trevor, who has provided some vital jogging of my memory over all this, reminds me that "F. Gilbert" was what he was always known as; none of us was ever sure of his first name! He was always such an elder statesman that nothing other than "Mr. Gilbert" ever seemed appropriate and Mr. Gilbert he always was.

Les, in his turn, co-opted Trevor and myself and I, of course, already knew something about the problems facing the Festiniog thanks to my day with Lord Northesk two years earlier. In the meantime, and unknown to me, the famous "Bristol Meeting" had taken place; nevertheless, at the end of a highly successful day out on the East Coast main line and much time spent either on the footplate or in propping up the bar of the Buffet Car, Trevor, Les and I were quite convinced we had a mission in life, namely, to do something about the Festiniog.

In January 1953 we all met at the Lion at Criccieth. I got there first, Trevor and Les rolling up at about 1 a.m. on a very cold Saturday. After a few hours' sleep we spent a rather dreary morning (it was obviously pouring, of course) inspecting Boston Lodge to the accompaniment of heavy drops of rain though the roof and the doleful prognostications of dear old Robert Evans. In the afternoon the weather improved a bit and we went up to Blaenau where we had the odd experience of hiring a FR slate wagon for 2/6d from a farmer who shall be nameless and bowling down to the tunnel by gravity. Bowl we did, too; when the tunnel mouth yawned black and menacing ahead of us we suddenly accelerated and seemed positively to shoot into the stygian darkness (yes, that's right; we'd overlooked the little matter of how to stop the darned thing). Eventually, of course, we did stop only to find water pouring down our necks from above and water several inches deep on the tunnel floor. We didn't exactly relish the idea of going on, so we made our way back the way we'd come. I think it's fair to say that despite getting very wet, and having had a full morning of prophesies of doom, we were all tremendously excited by what we had seen and when, next day, the Welsh weather did one of its incredible rapid changes and turned on positively springlike sunshine we were well and truly hooked.

Trevor's sister was married to a solicitor who had gone into industry rather than the law and whom I had known for some years. Although not a railway enthusiast in those days, he was intrigued to hear what we had seen and what Lord Northesk had told me more than 2½ years earlier about the apparent impossibility of doing anything about getting the railway going again due to all the legal complications. With the help of a friend of his at Rootes he set about seeing how a take-over of the Company could be brought about. After eighteen months' work, a tremendous amount of time and voluminous correspondence they had ironed out the problems and a take-over was possible. Those two heroes were the present Chairman, John Routly and E.D.Nicholson who is the Company's Registrar. It had been made clear that if the problems could be resolved I would find the money and although I did not have the ready cash available, my bank manager indicated that he was prepared to assist. However, to my great astonishment my father said he would let me have the necessary amount as an interest-free loan and that was what he did. My surprise at his generous gesture arose from the fact that he had bad hang-ups about Wales and the Welsh which stemmed from his not getting on with one of his brothers-in-law who was a Welshman; he made it absolutely clear that he had no intention of having anything to do with the railway once I had got control. He was as good as his word, and never did!

So it was that, in June 1954, the threads that had first come to my notice four years before, all eventually came together and on the 24th of that month the final formalities were completed. We held a Board Meeting, I became the Chairman and invited John Routly to be Deputy Chairman, since without him control would never have been gained. We were to remain unchanged in these positions for the next eighteen years. The other directors appointed at that time were Trevor Bailey, Les Smith and Bill Broadbent.

Needless to say, an awful lot had been going on in many other spheres of activity during those three years 1951-1954 and Trevor had got to know Allan Garraway. A few months after the new board had assumed control Trevor and Allan came up to Portmadoc for a weekend. That was in October 1954; let me quote Trevor's own words on the subject:

"It was shortly after he (i.e. Allan Garraway) and Bill Harvey had extracted the Simplex and a couple of coaches from Boston Lodge for the first time, and Allan was impatient to push on up the line. The undergrowth and brambles completely covered the line from outside Boston Lodge works to Minffordd and after taking stock of some wagons for disposal for scrap we collected the Simplex and set about the destruction of the undergrowth by charging into it until the loco was about to stall, backing up, and then removing the uprooted gorse and brambles by hand - an unpleasant task, but a rewarding one. By nightfall we had reached the upper end of Boston Lodge Halt area, where there was a nasty bank slip over which the track was suspended for about half its width. We had an early night (we'd set off that day at 3.30 a.m.) and returned to our labours at 6 a.m. By breakfast time we had jacked up the track, shored it with sleepers and taken the Simplex across the gap - known for some time afterwards as Bailey's Gap. So much progress was made that weekend that we were able to run an official train from Minffordd to Port in November on the occasion of the presentation to Robert Evans on his 60th anniversary with the railway and I feel that, in a small way, our efforts were something of a turning point".

I must say, I well remember that train. Goodness knows how the two passenger coaches had been got up to Minffordd, but going down there were branches of trees bashing against the windows and one or two actually broke. This was all the more embarrassing as I had invited our first guests, Sir Osmond and Lady Williams and their two small daughters, to join me as passengers; the little girls took a very dim view of the breaking glass and screamed their heads off! It's perhaps significant, and not altogether surprising, that both have vivid recollections to this day of that historic journey.

It was in those early days that policies evolved which were not unconnected with my experience in running special trains on British Railways. For example, the idea that every train should have an observation car and a licensed bar stemmed directly from my frequent use of the ex-Coronation Beaver Tails and, later, the Observation Cars from the Devon Belle whenever I could get hold of them in the knowledge that, when anything went wrong (as it often did!) one could suggest that everyone had a drink while waiting to be rescued.

The appointment of Allan Garraway as Manager (which is what he was to start with) bristled with problems, as he was one of the bright Young Men in the Motive Power Department of the Eastern Region and I was a part-time member of that region's board. To "steal" someone from the service of one's own senior officers presented a particularly delicate situation, not to mention the fact that Allan's father was himself a recently retired full time railwayman who knew all about working for the LNER but who clearly had grave reservations about his son chucking up a promising career with an established institution for a pie-in-the sky appointment which might work out, but equally well might not. It should be remembered that soon after control had been gained the news had broken that an abandoned hydro-electric scheme, which had at one time threatenend the line's route north of Dduallt, was being replaced by an even worse threat in the shape of Britain's first pumped storage scheme, and the viability of the whole take-over was called in question. Could a truncated railway be profitable? Would we get compensation? Could the proposed project be located elsewhere, even at this late stage, if we made representations? If not, could a diversion be built?

In the event, the powers-that-be of the Eastern Region bent over backwards to be helpful.

Allan was allowed to go his own way without undue difficulty and his father made it clear that he wasn't going to stand in his way either. Thus it was that Allan became the new administration's first salaried member of the staff.

The first battle in the war over the pumped storage scheme was an appeal before a select committee of the House of Lords which, in effect, said "can't Parliament persuade the Electricity people to flood some other valley instead?" and I was the one who had to appear before Their Lordships. There were five of them to one of me (if you see what I mean) and, because that particular hearing took place before we'd actually opened any part of the line to traffic, I could only quote all the things we were going to do without the advantage of being able to point to anything we'd actually done. Eloquent though I endeavoured to be, there was just no way I could get a scheme of that magnitude set aside or re-located, especially as its creation was going to benefit a depressed area where there was a high level of unemployment; as everyone knows, the Company's plea was rejected. It didn't do me any good personally, either, as the story was put about in some quarters that I was only interested in getting compensation for myself (in view of my having found the money for the take-over). Worse still, some even went so far as to suggest that I wasn't interested in opening the line again at all, but had organised the take-over knowing there was a problem on which I could cash in! Perhaps it was against this background that, a couple of years later, the Society demanded certain assurances about my intentions which resulted in this declaration:

"... Mr Pegler ... has no intention, nor is there any prospect of his 'lining his own pocket' as a result of the operations of the Railway Company".

To complete the story, that solemn declaration was contained in an official legal agreement between the Company, the Society and myself in March 1957.

Private, and not for Publication.

SOUTHERN RAILWAY

TRAFFIC MANAGER'S OFFICE,

GENERAL CIRCULAR No. 764.
                                           4th January, 1947.

INSTRUCTIONS TO ALL CONCERNED.

| GO LIGHTLY WITH THE LIGHT—**AND FUEL** |

CLOSING OF FESTINIOG RAILWAY.

8. The above railway has been closed; traffic for the places which it formerly served passing on G.W.R. accounts must be sent and invoiced as follows :—

Blaenau Festiniog	Send and invoice to Blaenau Festiniog G.W.R.
Dduallt	,, ,, ,, ,, ,, ,, ,,
Duffws	,, ,, ,, ,, ,, ,, ,,
Minffordd	,, ,, ,, ,, Minffordd G.W.R.
Penrhyndeudraeth	,, ,, ,, ,, Penrhyndeudraeth G.W.R.
Portmadoc	,, ,, ,, ,, Portmadoc G.W.R.
Tany-bwlch	,, ,, ,, ,, Maentwrog Rd. G.W.R. or Penrhyndeudraeth
Tany-grisiau	,, ,, ,, ,, Blaenau Festiniog G.W.R.

Commercial Supt's Ref. EP2/32496.

59. Much of the main yard was clear by the time that this photograph was taken on 23rd January 1955. The locomotive in traffic was kept on the right. (AGWG)

60. Termed a "Tourist" coach, this had been kept in Glan-y-Mor Yard, but was outside the loco shed in September 1954. (RWFS)

61. *September 1954 and initial clearance had taken place in the vicinity of Boston Lodge Halt. The loco shed and its two water tanks are in the background. (AGWG)*

62. *The same location and time as the previous photograph, but in the other direction, and there is little evidence of the cottages. (AGWG)*

63. By September 1954, further decay and theft had taken place at Minffordd. Lamps of this type were not collectible at that time. (AGWG)

64. The sunken siding in Minffordd Yard was heavily overgrown and was cleared to expedite the transfer of loco coal from BR. This is September 1955. (AGWG)

65. *Some of our contributors were on the first train to reach Minffordd; the date was 6th November 1954. Michael Davies is on the brake van platform, while Alan Pegler and F. Gilbert stand together at the left end of number 10. (RWFS)*

66. *Penrhyn station was in a sorry state by the time that it was recorded on 8th January 1955. (RWFS)*

❦ Rob Smallman ❧

In 1943 I had my first sight of the Talyllyn Railway, for I remember being put in a slate wagon full of straw with a picnic and travelling up the railway behind the train. We were parked in a siding and when the train passed by on the way down, we were told that we could come back in our own time. I do remember Dad having to push a bit, shouting when he had to run after us, as we picked up speed.

My time came for Boarding School in September 1946 and this was at Tavistock in Devon. Living in Birmingham at the time, it meant travelling down to Bristol by LMS, then change to GWR to Exeter, then swiftly over the bridge to catch the Southern Railway to Tavistock.

I draw a veil over the next four years, suffice to say I did very little work, because the classroom had windows on two sides. On one side you had the Southern Railway with the West Country Class thundering down to Plymouth and on the other side GWR tank engines gently pullng two coaches going to Launceston.

The Model Railway Show was at the Central Hall Westminster in 1952. Here I saw a narrow gauge slate wagon on a small piece of railway track, half had stones on, the rest had weeds; I looked at this and could not make out what it meant. A young man came up and asked me to join. "Join what", I said. He explained that I could work on a narrow gauge railway and get a magazine each quarter for £1. I could not get my money out fast enough. That, gentle reader, was my introduction to the Talyllyn Railway.

On 26th November 1952 I saw a newspaper cutting in the *Cambrian News*. Headlines "Race against time to save little Railway" with an address of a Mr Gilbert, secretary of the new Festiniog Railway who I wrote to at once, and joined.

In September 1954 I spent a leave from the RAF in Portmadoc. I walked miles either on the track or when impossible in the fields, until one morning feeling very brave, I tried to break into Boston Lodge. Just as I was thinking how to do it, a very gentle hand fell on my shoulder. Turning round I saw to my astonishment a dog collar which belonged, of course, to the self appointed guardian of Boston Lodge, Rev. Timmy Philips. Once I had told him of my interest, he produced a large key and took me into the works. What a treat was in store for me. I can still see round the old shop, in my imagination, just before going to sleep at night (what a sad person I am), even fifty odd years later.

Next day I met Allan Garraway for the first time, who was working on the Simplex. He pulled two coaches out on to the Cob for the local paper to take a photograph of Mr Evans who was still the manager there. I had met him a few days earlier in the huge office on the first floor of Harbour station. This strange little man from another age.

I was invited to join Allan the next day on a trip up the line, so complete with a picnic I went to find him. First of all, I found the wooden gates to Boston Lodge open and someone had dug out the sand from the points near an old wartime pillbox and on to the main line. The next obstacle was to find the gates at the top of the steps from the tollgate. I believe the old company paid a toll for any slate passing through the gate. I then passed the now quiet engine shed and the Rev. Philips house and under the road bridge, getting wet in the process. Then the cemetery and our first crossing gates. Here I met Leonard Heath Humphries and Michael Davies for the first time. The rails had been covered by the passage of time, although it was not tarmac so work was very slow. "You must be very thirsty, have a cup of tea" came a voice that I can still hear now, and there was Lottie, one of the kindest ladies I have ever met. She was living in the crossing keeper's house. Hours later we were through and on our way again, well perhaps 50 yards and the simplex was off the track. What now? Allan had all the tackle, crowbars, blocks of wood, a car jack, etc. What had happened was that in the undergrowth was a set of points from the long siding and they were half open. Getting the Simplex back on the rails was the end of our adventure for that day.

My next visit was on the 6th and 7th November 1954, when quite a gathering of people came for a journey for the first time to Minffordd Station. I sat with Mr Gilbert in one of the two carriages, with branches of trees smashing the glass windows as we travelled. Speeches by, I think, the Chairman of the Portmadoc council and a presentation to Mr Evans, the Railway Manager, who had completed 61 years service to the line. He started at a wage of 5/- (25p) a week. This was the first time that I met Alan Pegler, who entertained us at a buffet supper in the Queens Hotel. After that, weekends of working parties were held each month, all through the winter.

I was in the last months of my service with the RAF at Whitby and I would save up all my time off to have what was called a long weekend.

I left camp on the first bus into Whitby on a Friday morning and caught a train to Malton using what is now part of the North Yorkshire Moors Railway. I changed to a York train, then at York to a Birmingham train. Arriving in Birmingham New Street I was met by one of the family business employees and was driven at top speed to Snow Hill station. Here I caught a train to Ruabon, changing again to the Dee Valley line. We arrived at last at Portmadoc and walked to the Owens' Commercial Hotel for hot chocolate. Most times AGWG would come and say what the job was that weekend.

A hearty breakfast and a packed lunch would see us at the station soon after 9am. Now what we did each time is jumbled up in my mnd, but I do remember one Saturday, we managed to cross over the road at Penrhyn and started to move quickly along until we encountered a stone wall right across the track. This stumped us, but that evening, after a large dinner at Owens and a visit to one of the pubs, we decided to go very early next day and clear the line.

It must have been about 6am on the Sunday morning that we started off, on *Busta*, which belonged to Ian Smart. That was a hell ride; it only had two speeds - fast, and very fast. We demolished the wall. Well satisfied with our handy work we retired back to Port for breakfast. Passing by later on in the day the owner was rebuilding his wall back in the proper place, and gave us a cheery wave.

A cold supper was laid on for us at the Commercial, on the Sunday night, and I said good-bye to those who had to go. I had an early night, and after another large breakfast on Monday morning, paid my bill, which was 18/6d (90p) dinner/bed & breakfast and packed lunch. I walked down to the GWR station and caught the Cambrian Coast Expresss.

Arriving at Dovey Junction you could see the front half of the train coming from Aberystwyth. Once the train was joined up the restaurant car attendant would call out first or second lunch. Now here was another treat, for the Dining Car was only one coach, with the kitchen in the centre, and first and third class seating either side. Here again I got to know the crew, and sat in the First Class most of the time.

Arriving in Birmingham, a bus ride home, bath and tea, then down to New Street to catch the night train to York, connection being at some ungodly hour to Malton, and the milk train to Whitby. Bus up to the camp and in by 8am on Tuesday morning. I did this journey, I believe, six times.

I left the RAF at the end of August, and spent my terminal leave on the railway. By this time *Prince* was steaming and I was station master, ticket clerk, refreshment room attendant, guard and shunter. Then on the 9th September 1955 we had the national newspapers to record the 10,000th passenger, in fact a family from Birmingham. This was after the first 6 weeks of running.

During the winter of 1955 I was asked if it was possible to form a Midland Group of the Festiniog Railway, so armed with the members list I wrote to all local people and invited them to my parent's house in Edgbaston, Birmingham. This was the start of great friendships which still go on today. This then started a monthly working party, alternate to the London Group. One of the first things we did was to bring a wooden wagon back to the Midlands to rebuild as our homework. We were given a car showroom in West Bromwich to work in, and got lots of publicity for the railway.

At the first AGM to be held at Portmadoc, I was asked to join the Board of the FRS, to represent the Midlands, and at 21 years of age was very honoured to be in the company of such important railwaymen. That Autumn the Midland Group organised a large railway exhibition at Bingey Hall, Birmingham and *Welsh Pony* made a guest visit.

67. The Simplex trundles through Penrhyn with a working party in March 1955. By this time the station was used as a footpath. (RWFS)

68. Later in March 1955, the gates at Penrhyn were opened to allow the same train over the road. The FRS board debated automation of the crossing at this time. (RWFS)

69. The Simplex steams away merrily at Gysgfa, above Tan-y-Bwlch, in March 1955, as volunteers work above it. *(RWFS)*

70. Gravitating without brakes would seem to require some stamina. However, vegetation would keep Ian Smart under control at Rhiw Goch in February 1955 and pushing was often necessary. *(RWFS)*

❦ Ian Smart ❧

My first connection with the FR was in about 1930. I lived in Llandudno and my parents presented me with a 'Ten Bob Contract Ticket' which had two benefits. It got me from under my parents feet for a week and allowed me to roam around North Wales. I went to the limits of the ticket, Holywell, Holyhead, Amlwch, Afon Wen and Blaenau Festiniog. At the latter, I wandered out of the North Western Station, found the FR, noted the rails and the sheep and, as it was a typical Blaenau day, braved the rain and rejoined the LMS for Llandudno Junction.

Many years later, I holidayed in Criccieth and noticed the diagonal rail crossing in Port; in a 'sit up & beg' Ford one could hardly miss it. I settled the family the following day and had a look at the dereliction at Harbour Station. I walked across to Boston Lodge and effected an entry (Timmy Philips must have been shopping). I had a browse around and noticed the lamp on the Double Fairlie. Later, I discovered it was the Yankee Lamp off *Moelwyn*, modified with a stub of a candle therein.

In 1954 I found an article in the local paper about the potential rebuilding of the FR. I wrote to AGWG in the south and thus became a very early member.

I started work in late 1954, doing track clearance and so on, and had a very early trip from Tan-y-Bwlch towards Port. On December 18th Mike Davies and I set off with a slab wagon, loaded with a small saw and axe together with several bottles of R.M.Jones minerals. We made fair progress towards the area of Plas private station, having carved our way through a number of small trees and branches across the line ... we came to a larger tree across the line; our feeble efforts with the small tackle defeated us and we sat down somewhat exhausted. Shortly, a lone figure came down the line, John Young, complete with large cross cut saw and man size axe. He was through our obstacle in minutes and we managed to gravitate back to base. This was the first railed vehicle to travel down from Tan-y-Bwlch to Penrhyn since 1946.

One of our greatest steps forward at Boston Lodge was when Stan Salmon (a South Walian and electricity professional) connected Boston Lodge to the mains one gloomy evening. One 100-watt bulb and one 15-amp outlet was a vast improvement.

In early 1955 I took the remains of the Welsh Highland platelayers motorised trolley to Manchester and with the help of the Manchester Group rebuilt it. We found a horizontally opposed twin cylinder Petter air cooled engine and a motor bike gear box, with three forward and one reverse. The finished machine was a difficult starter, but when started was lethally fast.

Near Groeslon, Caernarvon, was former Welsh Highland Carriage no. 26. Allan Garraway asked me what I thought about recovering it to Boston Lodge. I weighed the job up as the carriage was fairly accessible. I called upon some of my friends in the Manchester area and managed to borrow a Bedford crane; brother-in-law in Scotland lent me a four-wheeled skeleton trailer. One weekend we assembled the gear and the old gang, Fred Boughey, John Halsall and a few others whose names I forget. After loading we brought the lot to Harbour station where Allan G had organised a pair of bogies. We dropped 26 on the bogies and the Simplex brought the lot to Boston Lodge.

FESTINIOG RAILWAY.
Notice.- This Ticket is issued subject to the conditions on the Time Tables of the Company.
PORTMADOC
TO
TANY GRISIAU
FIRST CLASS Fare 2s. 6d
417

71. A stop for a brief respite on Cei Mawr was recorded in March 1955. The undergowth had been severe above this location. (RWFS)

72. AGWG, LAHH and AMD discover "an unexpected crossover with blades at half cock", on 23rd October 1954. (RWFS)

❧ Bob Smith ❧

I was taken on holiday to North Wales by my parents in 1939 and that included a ride on the FR. I can clearly recall waiting at Tan-y-Bwlch for a train and seeing a double engine. Strangely I don't know which way we went - if going up to Blaenau the journey through the old Moelwyn tunnel would probably have been pretty frightening for a small child. However, this is my earliest memory and perhaps had something to do with my ongoing railway interests.

In 1954 news of the serious revival efforts on the FR became public and I expressed my interest and offered to help if possible. I heard that things might actually be happening on the ground in September of that year, so I booked some leave, I was doing my National Service at the time, and was present when the Simplex and a couple of carriages made the first run across the Cob since 1946. I distinctly recall helping move a plaster relief model of the railway from Boston Lodge across to Harbour Station for safe keeping. What has become of that? There was track across Brittania Bridge then and I remember Allan Garraway taking the Simplex as far as possible to get it near the garage to save carrying petrol too far, also a puzzled AA patrolman stopping to look at it!

My next visit was in February 1955 for a week when I met Bob Smallman and among other things we were given the task of re-railing a carriage in the works yard. We also cleared rubbish from the track behind the houses in Glan-y-pwll to enable access to Blaenau and retrieve wagons. At that time the shed at Glan-y-Pwll was used by a timber merchant, as was Minffordd goods shed. My National Service finished at Easter 1955, and I spent my demob leave on the FR. I 'lived' in a carriage in the old loco shed and was accompanied by my cousin Peter Bailey. We did some trackwork out on the Cob. The procedure was 'new' sleepers under the joints (these were ex BR which we cut up ourselves, no chain saws or indeed any other power tools) and one or two others per rail length. Some rails had to be replaced where the webs had rusted through. Another job was digging out an amount of sand from under the line just above Boston Lodge Halt. The Revd Timmy Philips was a self appointed guardian of the Works and he paid for a lorry load of ballast to be delivered when we relaid that short length.

Mentioning Timmy Philips reminds me of all the other old characters who were around then: Tom Davies (I stayed with him and his wife for Bed & Breakfast a few times), Will and Bessie Jones at Tan-y-Bwlch, Lottie Edwards at Minffordd, Morris Jones in the Works and Robert Evans who was still Manager at that time.

Since those early days I have worked on the FR almost every year for over 50 years and made many good and long-lasting friendships. I have worked on the majority of the line at some time, including taking out the WHR connection at the Harbour, working in the new Moelwyn Tunnel, lifting the track from Dduallt to the old tunnel, on the track around the 'new' shed at Glan-y-Pwll and several times in Blaenau station.

FESTINIOG RAILWAY.

Notice,- This Ticket is issued
subject to the conditions on the
Time Tables of the Company.

MINFFORD JUNCTION
TO
PENRHYN

FIRST CLASS Fare 6d.

363

73. A pause was made for a photograph at Tan-y-Bwlch on a trip up the line on 28th May 1955. AGWG is driving. (RWFS)

74. Tan-y-Bwlch was recorded from near the top points in September 1954. Grazing kept the vegetation under control here. (RWFS)

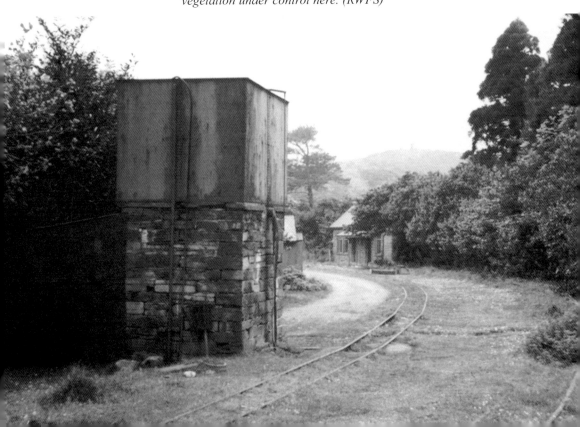

✑ John Snell ✑

I first explored the Festiniog Railway during the Easter 1947 school holidays, hoping to find that the news paragraphs in the *Railway Magazine* were all wrong and that life remained. They were not wrong; but the track lay open and unobstructed all the way from Blaenau G.W.R. to Port. Here and there the drains were choked and a few bushes and brambles would have rubbed against the coaches. In fact it took some nerve to walk through the long tunnel; there was no reason why a train might not have come along, and getting caught half-way down the rat-hole would not have been funny. I had just travelled for the first time on the Talyllyn Railway, then in its state of awesome decrepitude, and I was very much struck by the contrast. If the T.R. could still run the Festiniog had obviously just copped out. Gutless!

Four years later, having left school, I found myself one of that small band led by Tom Rolt and David Curwen, setting the Talyllyn to rights. We had our hands full; but we were of course interested in the rumours of strange resurrection activities going on further north, and we made several expeditions to have a look. I remember getting quite excited by obvious signs of recent use on the rails at Tan-y-Bwlch, and the line above was still temptingly clear and, by T.R.standards, in excellent order. But it all came to nothing at that stage.

We made several other graveyard inspections over the next few years, but it was not till March 1954, by then free of my commitment to the Talyllyn, that I decided to explore the remains thoroughly with a friend, Peter Barlow, who went on subsequently to a career in B.R. management. We therefore settled into the "North Western Hotel" in Blaenau for a few days with a large stock of 35mm film. We were pretty lucky with the weather, and extended our stay to take in journeys to, and over the whole of, the Dinorwic system as well as the Llandudno & Colwyn Bay.

Blaenau itself was fascinating, and two whole days were hardly enough. We saw and photographed the Oakeley Lister working traffic over the F.R. to the two standard-gauge stations, and photographed, less successfully, the extraordinary twin-pole electric locomotive at Llechwedd. We saw and photographed some of the complex pointwork in the Oakeley quarry, adapted to double-flanged wagon wheels of variable gauge; men cutting and splitting slates; incline working as it should be; and we just missed seeing incline working as it should not. Llechwedd had a runaway on the incline leading down to the wharf at the end of the B.R. tunnel while we were there. We heard it and we saw the cloud of dust, but it seemed tactless to photograph the wrecked wagons and broken slates.

Quite a lot of slate was still despatched from Blaenau by rail, from both stations, and narrow-gauge slate wagons belonging to G.W.R. and L.N.W.R. were still in use. The old G.W.R transporter trucks, used to carry narrow-gauge wagons from Manod to Blaenau, were still there but derelict.

We spent another day walking the line from Blaenau to Tan-y-Bwlch. Seven years had made a difference. The way was still clear, but more cuttings were water-logged and there did not seem to be a single key to hold the rails anywhere between the L.N.W. station and the tunnel. We supposed that they had gone for firewood. Some of the underbridges looked dangerous, and there were some wrecked wagons teetering above the water on a bridge on the Dinas branch to emphasise the fact. The tunnel was more sinister than ever, with broken steel grids at the bottom of the air shafts and heaps of rocks on the track which had fallen through them. But everything was still there, just as it had been left 20 or 30 years earlier, even the Cwmorthin Quarry tramway above Tanygrisiau and, so far as we could see through the boarded windows, all the equipment in the sheds.

I would not have trusted some of the wire ropes on the inclines, but with a little clearance and, of course, the will and the money, it all looked as if work and production of slate could re-start next Monday. But the enormous appeal of this most spectacular part of the Railway was very strong, and best of all there were signs of life. Wagons had been pushed along between Tanygrisiau and Tunnel Cottage, at the north end of the Moelwyn Tunnel and still occupied, and between Tan-y-Bwlch and Coed-y-Bleiddiau, which was also regularly inhabited. Of course neither of these houses had any means of access except walking. The oddest discovery was a small tortoise, steadily plodding uphill along the track near Dduallt Manor. We had a lot of odd animals on the line at Talyllyn but never a tortoise, and I have a photograph to prove it.

Next day was much heavier work. We took the bus from Blaenau to the Oakeley Arms, then set about walking from Tan-y-Bwlch to Portmadoc. The weather had broken as well so showers of rain made things no easier. Brushwood on the track below Tan-y-Bwlch steadily turned into dense thickets. Quite soon we came across the bogie wagon that somebody had recently ridden down the grade from Blaenau; their speed had blasted them into the middle of a patch of jungle and there it stayed. When we got into the rhododendron country by what is now Plas Halt the track was often invisible, and it was a real struggle to continue. Further on young trees grew thickly between the sleepers. Little of the view could be seen and one was tempted to escape along one of the hill paths that crossed the line from time to time. But we battered on, seeing signs that others had done the same, and at last, when we got to the Cae Mawr, we reached tolerably open country again. It has grown up round the Railway much more in recent years along this section. The Cae Mawr then still looked like a solid stone viaduct.

I photographed two items along this section that seemed to have been forgotten: a strange hand-operated dwarf disc signal at Penrhyn level crossing whose purpose seemed obscure. The crossing keeper must have used it to signal trains, but why bother? They would not have seen the disc until long after they could see whether the gates were open or not. The other one was the full-size disc signal on the Minffordd side of what later became known as "Lottie's Crossing", which stood on a cast-iron pole, ten feet high, and looked like one of Brunel's cast-offs. Except for the famous three-way signal at Portmadoc and one just above the level crossing at Glan-y-Pwll (Blaenau L.N.W.) I cannot remember any other surviving FR semaphore signals, so it was extraordinary to find these two relics from a much earlier era. By the time we reached Penrhyn that day, however, we were too shattered to start another fight against the undergrowth as the line became blocked again, so we walked along the road as far as Minffordd. Having examined the rather splendid Cleminson six-wheeled covered van (better known in its later form as an open coal truck), which was among the bushes in the sidings above Lottie's Crossing, we called it a day and caught the bus back to Blaenau.

I had written some time before to Robert Evans, the Manager and last surviving employee of the Railway, asking for an appointment to see Boston Lodge Works.

He showed us some of his cluttered empire in the Harbour Station and he presented us with some single-line tickets for the Portmadoc (New) to Croesor Junction section of the W.H.R. He then crossed over to Boston Lodge and opened up. It was an amazing and pathetic sight, often enough described, and I cannot add to what has been said about it before, except again to mourn *Moel Tryfan* which stood under the falling roof of the loco shed alongside one of the Fairlies. You always regret the ones that get away.

75. Work was underway near Penrhyn back on 7th November 1954, but few residents were interested. (AGWG)

76. This is the situation at Bryn Mawr after a path had been cleared for the initial inspection. (RWFS)

77. *The track was always reasonably clear in the vicinity of Garnedd Tunnel, as evident in September 1954. The original route is visible on the right. (RWFS)*

78. *The upper end of Garnedd Tunnel was equally clear when photographed, also in September 1954. The bar across the track once carried ropes to remind brakesmen to sit down. (AGWG)*

*79. Very few photos were taken in 1946 but this one of **Prince** above Tan-y-Bwlch by Revd. B. Williams shows marks on the chairs due to flange impact.*

80. The Simplex was recorded at the north end of Moelwyn Tunnel in April 1955. The siding to Brookes Quarry is on the left and its points are on the right. Also on the right was a GPO letterbox. (JBS)

81. Tanygrisiau is in the distance in this view from close to the site on which the power station was built. (KC)

82. Tanygrisiau station and its environs changed little and its generous canopy remained until after the track was lifted. (KC)

❧ Dan Wilson ❧

In 1948 my father organised a walk from Blaenau to Penrhyn. Blaenau was an horrifically sour place: the hostility to any kind of outsider, not just English but coastal Welsh too, positively oozed from the stones. People from other parts of Wales put this down to inbreeding, no sunshine during the winter and poor diet, but I believe it was an extreme example of America effect. The more enterprising people in a community will always move away if there are better prospects elsewhere and Blaenau's especial characteristic was that it was somewhere cheap to live with absolutely zero prospects.

Having peered over Queen's Bridge at the still operative leased section, we started at Stêsion Fain. The main line had been barred aside at one joint to prevent runaways making off for Glan-y-Pwll gates, but otherwise the FR was clear and workable all the way to Moelwyn Tunnel, though sawdust covered the track opposite Glan-y-Pwll Yard which was rented by a timber company. Tanygrisiau station was occupied and in reasonable fettle and the complete junctions for Cwmorthin and Wrysgan inclines were in place. I am told that around this period Wrysgan incline was reopened as a powered single line. A Hudson skip was padlocked to the main line at Tanygrisiau. At Doppog, more or less where the power station now is, we heard a clanging behind us and beheld this vehicle bearing down on us, carrying the occupant of Tunnel Cottage, sitting sideways and punting it along with her legs. Its rear axle was severely bent, so as it passed it bobbed like a frightened sheep. We shortly came across a cornflake packet lying in the two-foot (?) and gravely handed it in at the cottage. Inside the tunnel mouth a shallow pile of stones prevented the trolley from overshooting, but it had recently been disturbed and we found the reason for this at Dduallt, where a half-full coal wagon stood in the siding. Again the Railway was clear and workable from here on to the top end of Tan-y-Bwlch station, where chicken wire obstructed it. Here Will and Bessie Jones reigned over an empire. A goat was tethered to a rail and accounted for the generally mown appearance of the track-bed.

At the bottom end of Tan-y-Bwlch station there remained two coal wagons remnants of Will's small coal-merchanting during the war. The larger one of these was mobile and I was permitted to ride up and down on it until Bessie appeared to make sure we were not proposing to take it to Portmadoc with us. She still did teas but not on a commercial basis - only for those people who called in out of curiosity and expressed an interest.

Had a slate gravity train been run down at this time from Dduallt (and forgetting the chicken wire) I estimate that it would have come to a decided stop just below Whistling Curve. Here the saplings were man high (we had lunch and I took a photo) and thenceforth to Rhiw Goch it was a matter of following the pathway kept open by walkers. There, that came to an end and we transferred to the fields, not being aware of the farm road that runs parallel. I felt downcast - the Festiniog had this air of being something superior in ruins, like an Egyptian temple.

In 1949 we walked up from Tan-y-Bwlch to Blaenau, but went over the tunnel to avoid the hysterics our dog had had in it the previous year. Rhoslyn was by then unoccupied but the coal wagon remained. As a result of "maintenance" by sheep, Dduallt looked identical 15 years later when the Deviation was started. Tunnel Cottage had lost its trolley, but we noticed that there was another one behind a wall at Buarth Melyn. By now rubbish was beginning to be dumped on the track in Blaenau. We hoped for a second visit to Votty & Bowydd quarry, but it was on short time and no-one was around.

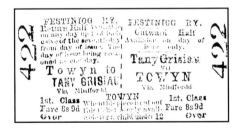

92

83. *An anxious moment was recorded on 5th February 1955 as Simplex crept across the partially cleared Glan-y-Pwll crossing for the first time. (RWFS)*

84. *The second visit of Simplex to Glan-y-Pwll was on 5th March 1955. The entire area was very neglected at this period. (RWFS)*

85. A later trip to the top of the line was for scrap collection, when a BR van was delayed by Simplex. (KC)

86. The posters concerning the plan to reopen were posted in June 1955; Rob Smallman is doing so with great pride. (RWFS)

❧ POSTSCRIPTS ❧

Both my grandparents had their roots in North Wales but had moved to Liverpool in the 19th century in search of work. Pre-war holidays were spent in Flintshire, travelling by train to Star Crossing or Nannerch, and I would be taken up Moel Fammau to look across the Vale of Clwyd to distant Snowdonia. I must have been told of the train which climbed Snowdon, for I fondly imagined that the plume of steam from the train travelling from Ruthin to Denbigh was that of the rack railway! Another pre war holiday was spent on the west coast of the Isle of Man where the morning train crossing the Glen Mooar viaduct was a wonderful introduction to the narrow gauge. Yes, my love for railways and all things Celtic must certainly be in the genes!

During my National Service years 1952-54 I made several visits whilst on leave, availing of free and reduced rate 'Forces' tickets, and it was at this period that my notice was drawn to a paragraph in the Liverpool Daily Post outlining plans for the 'Pegler' takeover. There was also a lovely pre war picture of a Down passenger train near Wrysgan Siding, Tan-y-Grisiau, a picture I had not previously seen.

The Festiniog Railway has been very much part of my life now for nearly sixty years, and a walk up Cwm Croesor in 1955 brought me in contact with Welsh friends where, years later I was to meet my wife. Six wonderful decades indeed!

Michael Davies

The revival scheme for the FR has brought as a by-product for Barbara and I many long lasting friendships, a great blessing indeed. Of particular pleasure has been the warm bond with several Merioneth people. We recognised from the outset the importance of involving local volunteers at the start of the action. The zero response and the inability of local employees to enthuse their brethren has been a disappointment. The same reaction to the front page presentation of the scheme at Easter 1955 was a surprise and a mystery.

However, equally amazing was the distance that others were prepared to travel in order to help bring back to life this incomparable part of Britain's heritage. Sadly many of those invited to contribute to this volume have been unable to do so. but our thanks go most sincerely to those who have. We must also be grateful for those who had the foresight to write in times past.

To bring together these memories has been our objective; we hope that the result is both enlightening and enjoyable, even if there has inevitably been some repetition of details.

Vic Mitchell

Middleton Press

EVOLVING THE ULTIMATE RAIL ENCYCLOPEDIA

Easebourne Lane, Midhurst, West Sussex.
GU29 9AZ   Tel:01730 813169

www.middletonpress.co.uk   email:info@middletonpress.co.uk
A-0 906520   B-1 873793   C-1 901706   D-1 904474

OOP Out of print at time of printing - Please check availability   BROCHURE AVAILABLE SHOWING NEW TITLES